WISDOM

Wisdom's Daughters

Stories of Women around Jesus

ELIZABETH G. WATSON

The Pilgrim Press
Cleveland, Ohio

The Pilgrim Press, Cleveland, Ohio 44115
© 1997 by Elizabeth G. Watson

Biblical quotations are from the New Revised Standard Version of the Bible,
© 1989 by the Division of Christian Education of the National Council of the
Churches of Christ in the U.S.A., and are used by permission

02 01 00 99 98 97   5 4 3 2 1

Library of Congress Cataloging-in-Publication Data

Watson, Elizabeth G.
    Wisdom's daughters : stories of women around Jesus /
Elizabeth G. Watson.
        p. cm.
    Includes bibliographical references.
    ISBN 0-8298-1221-0 (pbk. : alk. paper)
    1. Women in the Bible.   2. Jesus Christ—Friends and
associates. 3. Bible. N.T.—Biography.   I. Title.
BS2445.W37 1997
226'.0922'082—dc21   97-23171
                                                        CIP

In memory of my mother
Grace Edith Norvell Grill
my grandmothers
Sarah Elizabeth Barnum Norvell
Anna Elizabeth Qualman Grill
and my mother-in-law
Margaret Elizabeth Moore Watson

Contents

❦

Preface

❦

My interest in the women around Jesus goes back a long way. I had a call to the ministry early in my childhood, and that has shaped not only the inner events of my life but to a large extent the outer ones as well. Yet when I shared my good news with people, I did not receive encouragement. I was sometimes told that if Jesus had wanted women to be ministers and priests, he would have called women to be his disciples. I was fortunate that my father kept telling me, "Don't let anyone set limits on your ambition." When I began speaking in churches in high school, he let me know that he was proud of me.

I have been a Bible reader all my life, and I tried to connect with the women around Jesus, but they did not come fully alive for me until a half century after my original calling, when I reread the Gospels with feminist eyes. The book in its present form began in the spring of 1984 when I taught a course on women in the New Testament at Woodbrooke College, Birmingham, England. We read the Gospel stories aloud, compared different translations, filled in details from research and imagination, and brainstormed what the women's lives might have been like. Sometimes we role-played the stories.

The women stepped forth from the pages of the Gospels as real human beings whose lives were changed by their contact with Jesus. Their stories often seemed like parables of our own lives. Maxine Linnell, one of the group, said, "We build upon their lives. Their struggles make us strong. We too can sing their half-forgotten songs." Since then, in workshops and other groups on both sides of the Atlantic, I have watched people respond to the vitality of these women.

The idea grew in me to make a collection of the women's stories in chronological order. I began to tell the stories in the third person, but it soon became apparent that the women wanted to speak for themselves. Their stories are of necessity filtered through my experience and imagination, and I have not always been able to limit them to a vocabulary appropriate to women two thousand years ago. And the women sometimes comment on and throw light on my own contemporary concerns. As they became part of my life, I in some measure became part of theirs.

The book is a continuous story of the life of Jesus, pieced together from the four Gospels to be as consistent as possible. The story line is carried in a brief scriptural reference at the beginning of each chapter. Then follows a story told by a woman who was there. Some women in the early chapters cannot complete their stories, for to do so would push the main story line too far ahead. They appear later in other women's chapters so that their lives are not left dangling. The fourteen stories are thus to some extent interlocking. It seems reasonable that many of these women must have known one another.

Once I got into the writing, the logic of the book took over. I found that two of the major stories had to be told in flashbacks, because the primary woman involved, Mary the Mother, is so important in later events that her story cannot be told early in the book. The birth of Jesus, and his experience when he was twelve in the Temple in Jerusalem are told in flashbacks. The final chapter belongs to Mary, looking back at the end of her life and picking up details of other stories.

The Gospels were written by men and are largely about men. Until the twentieth century, they were edited, translated, and interpreted almost entirely by men. As I read and reread the Gospels, both in Greek and in various English translations, I

am convinced that the stories were often edited, and in some
measure rewritten, to minimize the role of the women. Gospels not in the canon, such as the Gnostic Gospels discovered
in the twentieth century, make it clear that women, particularly Mary Magdalene, played far larger roles than we have
been led to believe from the canonical Gospels.

As one sees Jesus interacting with the women, we watch
him calling them to follow him. In the end we see him en-
trusting his message to them, because the men, with the ex-
ception of John, have all deserted him. We find him breaking
virtually every taboo against women in his own day. I want to
absolve Jesus from any responsibility for the effort of the Christian Church to "keep women in their place."

One of the questions I faced early in the writing was which
English translation of the New Testament to use as the basic
text. I was disappointed in the New Revised Standard Version
when it came out, for though it made great strides in render-
ing much of the Bible into inclusive language, the decision
was made to keep "kingdom of God" and "Son of Man," and to
call Jesus "Lord" in many instances. However, by default, it
seemed in the end the best choice.

I did not want to use the word "kingdom," because I believe
Jesus was thinking of something much more egalitarian. After
all, he called his disciples "friends." A number of contemporary scholars use the word "reign" to express the length of
time or "realm" to express the geographic expanse of "the kingdom of God." I felt I could be comfortable using either of
those words. Then I hit upon "the commonwealth of God,"
which accurately describes the early band of Christians whose
stories are told in the Book of Acts. However, a dear friend, a
black South African woman, asked me not to use the word
"commonwealth" because of its negative connotations for
people on the African continent.

Marie Schutz of Santa Rosa, California, suggested to me
the word "community," and it seemed right. "Community" was
a key word and concept when I was studying process theology

at the University of Chicago Divinity School in the mid-1930s. It has continued to be a key word for me as I have worked out my calling to ministry over the years. For some time I worked as a community organizer in an interracial neighborhood in Chicago. At times, my husband and I have lived in intentional communities. As I have shared the stories with various groups, most people have felt that "community of God" sounded right. I was interested to discover that Nancy Mairs, in her book *Ordinary Time,* went through the same intellectual process that I went through and also came out with the phrase "the community of God."[1]

My method of working on the stories has been to pull together details from the different Gospels and to relate them to historical events and relevant archeological and geographic evidence. When my husband and I traveled in Israel, I consciously looked at landscapes to get a feel for the places where the stories happened.

I have visualized each woman as a whole person, acting and reacting to the situation in which she finds herself. I have consciously tried to follow the process used by a responsible historical novelist in filling out the historical record with details that are true to the life of the times. Sometimes, as in the story of the woman at the well, the Gospel account is quite full, and I have only added details to make it hang together. Occasionally other factual information in the Bible seems to relate to a story, and I have made the connection, as in the chapter on Joanna. Some Gospel references are so scant that the story comes almost wholly out of my imagination, as is the case with the woman who anointed Jesus. At the end of each story I have added my rationale in a section called "Comments."

Walt Whitman also contributes to my method. In his long poem "Out of the Cradle Endlessly Rocking," he recalls his first boyhood encounter with death, as he watched a nest of mockingbirds day after day, even night after night. The story itself is preceded by a fifteen-line catalog of elements of the narrative, pieces of memory assembled almost randomly, the

raw material for what follows. Then come these Whitmanesque
lines:

> I, chanter of pains and joys, uniter of here and hereafter,
> Taking all hints to use them, but swiftly leaping beyond them,
> A reminiscence sing.[2]

So I have combed the Gospel narratives for details, "hints,"
as Whitman calls them. My stories live or fall flat in propor-
tion to how high and how gracefully I can leap beyond the
details of the bare canonical stories, and how faithful I remain
to the women who have entrusted their stories to me.

There is another dimension to my method. In Genesis,
Yahweh brings the animals and other creatures to the man to
give them names, "and whatever the man called every living
creature, that was its name" (Gen. 2:19b). Ursula Le Guin
wrote a short story in which Eve unnames them.[3] I want to
carry that a step further. I see Eve then sitting down with
each living being, waiting for it to reveal its name to her. My
method of writing has been something like that. I have lived
with each woman in turn, waiting for her to reveal her story
to me.

And as I have lived with these women and experienced the
way Jesus changed their lives, I found him becoming more
deeply part of my own life. The stories he told, the stories told
about him, and above all the timelessness of what he taught
all came to me freshly. It was no longer familiar biblical passages I have known since childhood, but a wisdom particularly relevant to and needed in our own chaotic times.

Was it an accident that the women seemed to grasp what
he was saying more quickly than the men? that they did not
desert him in the end? that he entrusted his message to them?
Or did he speak their language, and understand their experience?

I reread the passage in the eighth chapter of Proverbs about
Wisdom (Sophia), co-creator of the universe, and definitely a

female figure. I turned to the first chapter of John's Gospel and saw how he borrowed ideas from the Wisdom figure in the Hebrew Scriptures and applied them to Jesus. He did not call Jesus *Wisdom,* but rather the *Logos,* the "Word": "And the Word became flesh and lived among us" (John 1:14)—bringing to us the Word, the Wisdom, of God.

Luke, speaking of the boy growing up in Nazareth, says, "And Jesus increased in wisdom and in years, and in divine and human favor" (Luke 2:52). When Jesus was a young man and preached in his home synagogue in Nazareth, Matthew records that the people asked, "Where did this man get this wisdom?" (Matt. 13:54b). And Paul speaks of "Jesus, who became for us wisdom from God" (1 Cor. 1:30b).

Many of the men did come to understand his message and gave their lives as witnesses to it. But there were women who did not have to grow into an understanding, who grasped immediately and intuitively what he said, and gave their lives into his keeping. They became Wisdom's Daughters. I seek to be one of them.

Acknowledgments

꙳

These stories began to take shape during 1983–84, when my husband, George, and I spent the academic year as Fellows at the Quaker Adult Study Center at Woodbrooke College, in Birmingham, England. In the spring of that year I taught a course on women in the New Testament. Christina Lawson, Librarian of Woodbrooke College, generously gave both professional and personal support during the class and has continued gentle transatlantic prodding in the years since, urging me to complete the book. My thanks and love go to her and also to three other British women, Val Ferguson, Jo Farrow, and Janet Scott, who have taken a special interest in the project and joined the prodding to complete the book.

After we returned to the United States, I used Jesus and the women around him as the subject of numerous workshops, lectures, and study groups across the North American continent.

In August 1990, at the annual regional gathering of Quakers known as the New England Yearly Meeting of Friends, five of the stories were given as the Bible half-hours: Elizabeth, Joanna, The Woman at the Well, The Mother of the Sons of Zebedee, and The Woman Who Anointed Jesus. Approximately 250 tapes of these stories have been sold since that summer.

The tape of The Woman Who Anointed Jesus was made into a small pamphlet under the title *The Crone* by the Wider Quaker Fellowship, and sent to their membership as part of their December 1990 mailing. The pamphlet was not copyrighted.

George and I spent the spring term of 1995 as Friends in Residence at Pendle Hill, the Quaker Center for Study and Contemplation in Wallingford, Pennsylvania, the American counterpart of Woodbrooke College. The fourteen stories, by then largely in their final form, were given as the Monday Evening Public Lecture Series. Somewhere between fifty and seventy-five copies of the eight tapes of those lectures were sold in the year following.

Many people have contributed their ideas and support and I am grateful for all the interest and encouragement I have received, although I can mention the names of relatively few people.

My special thanks and love go to Elizabeth Yeats, Religious Education and Publications Coordinator of Friends General Conference in Philadelphia, who personally committed herself to helping me get the book into final shape and published. Her constant belief in the worth of the manuscript saw me through periods of doubt.

Many other people have given generously of their time and their knowledge. In 1990 Judith Applegate, a New Testament scholar, and in 1993, Marian D. Hall, a psychologist, listened to me outline the book at some length, and both made helpful comments from their professional backgrounds.

Judith Applegate, McGregor Gray, Larry Naber, Marie Schutz, and Anne Thomas made specific suggestions that are noted in the Comments of the particular chapters in which they appear.

Marian Hall, William Kreidler, Sandy Olson, and Elizabeth Yeats read and commented helpfully on the final draft of the manuscript.

When the stories were beginning to take shape we were living in Easton, Massachusetts, and a group met in our home every two weeks in 1990–91 to study the Gospel records and discuss my ideas. My thanks and love to the members of this group—Charlotte Blaschke, Janet Billerbeck, Barbara Brooks, Jeanne Clepper, Martha Gordon, Kay Jeffery, Jesse Jones-Cobb, Ann and Bill Kriebel, Ilse Reich, Patricia Shotwell, Eunice Smith, Virginia Towle, Polly Wood, and Betty and Charles Woodbury.

In 1992 we moved to Minneapolis and became part of the Minneapolis Friends Meeting. In 1994 I asked the Meeting for a support group to listen to the drafts of the stories, now nearing completion. I asked them to be utterly honest and ruthless in their reactions, and they were! Much revision resulted. My special thanks to Patricia McKernon, who took notes of the discussions so that I could participate fully. My thanks and love to this group: Ranae Hanson, Patricia Jones, Jane Lund, Joan Matthews, Patricia McKernon, Sandy Olson, David Runkle, and Regula Russelle.

George and I were Friends in Residence at Pendle Hill in the spring of 1995 when the lecture series of the completed book took place. The entire community, staff and students, and many people from the area, were supportive and encouraging and concerned to see the book published. I thank them all.

Another member of Minneapolis Friends Meeting, Dan Lundquist, came to my rescue when my computer flashed increasingly urgent but enigmatic messages at me, and was especially helpful when the old computer finally died and had to be replaced in the middle of the final preparation of the book for the publisher.

Finally, my thanks and love to George, with whom I have shared the last sixty years. When the pressure of writing has been on me, he has cheerfully prepared meals, done the laundry, and kept the house running. He has been part of many of the groups discussing the stories, and can probably repeat from memory the text of every chapter with all its variations over the years. As with all the projects of my life, it is impossible to imagine the completion of this one without his unfailing love and support.

CHAPTER I

Elizabeth

Luke 1

*

In the days of King Herod of Judea, there was a priest
named Zechariah, who belonged to the priestly order of
Abijah. His wife was a descendant of Aaron, and her name
was Elizabeth. Both of them were righteous before God,
living blamelessly according to all the commandments. . . .
But they had no children . . . and both were getting on in
years.

—LUKE 1:5–7

The angel Gabriel was sent by God to a town in Galilee
called Nazareth, to . . . Mary. . . . The angel said to her, "Do
not be afraid, Mary, for you have found favor with God. And
now you will conceive in your womb and bear a son, and you
will name him Jesus." . . . Mary said to the angel, "How can
this be?"

—LUKE 1:26, 27b, 30–31, 34

In those days Mary set out and went with haste to a Judean
town in the hill country, where she entered the house of
Zechariah and greeted Elizabeth. . . . And Elizabeth was
filled with the Holy Spirit and exclaimed with a loud cry,
"Blessed are you among women."

—LUKE 1:39–40, 41b–42a

Elizabeth's Story

I have lived all my life in a little village in the hill country of Judea, about five miles west of Jerusalem. It is not on the main road that runs along the Jordan River, so traders and travelers do not often come. You won't find it on the map, but it is a good place to live. I love to climb the hill behind our house just before sunset. I can see the Holy City in the distance, its towers shining in the sun. *Jerusalem the golden, city of our God.*

My father was descended from Aaron and therefore was a member of the hereditary priesthood. I was named for Aaron's wife, Elisheba. You know me by the Greek form of my name, Elizabeth. The name means "worshiper of God," a meaning deeply important to me, for that is my way of life. As a child I felt God's presence with me almost constantly, and I talked to God quite simply.

Now, as an adult, I sometimes have to make a conscious effort to become quiet inside, to recall myself to God's presence. But it is always there and available to me. As a child, when I worked with my mother, I thought of my work as an offering to God, and now in my own house, I am conscious of the presence of God as I work. I feel that presence in everything: trees, water, hills, birds, animals, people, and especially in the stars. God is especially close to me under the night sky.

We have a tradition of angels in our religion. They are visible messengers of God and symbols of God's presence in the world. Often I seem to catch sight of bright wings in the distance as I roam the hills around our village.

Girls cannot go to the synagogue school, but my father taught me to read. I learned passages of scripture without much effort, and it has been a great resource all my life, living water in dry seasons, comfort in times of illness, and strength when decisions must be made. Had I been a man, I would have been a priest. When I was young, I resented being a girl, with all the limitations put upon me, but I am grateful now to be a woman. I have always wanted to be a channel for God's peace and love to flow to everyone.

When I was still a girl, I was married to a young priest named Zechariah. He belonged to a different priestly division from that of my father. He was a good man, devout, upright, earnest, but also tender, and with a sense of humor too. He had a magnificent voice, and when he read from Isaiah, it might have been the prophet himself speaking. Most important, he has always loved me, whatever has happened, and I have loved him, and our love has kept growing with all we have shared over the years.

I cannot remember a time when I did not know him and his family. Our many common memories were always a bond. In some ways, however, we were quite different. Zechariah loved the day; he rose early, worked hard, and when darkness came, he went to sleep quickly and slept soundly. Night is my time. We often slept on the roof in warm weather, with the great parade of stars overhead. God was so close to me then that sleep seemed a sacrilege.

Zechariah loved the law of Moses and meditated on it constantly, concerned to live out every detail. God spoke to him through the Torah. He did not understand my direct experience of God. He thought my angels the product of an overactive imagination. We saw the world and experienced reality differently. Sometimes it was a source of misunderstanding, but more often we laughed at our differences and put up with one another's peculiarities. Dear Zechariah! He's been gone a dozen years now. How much I miss him!

In spite of our happiness, we had one great sorrow: we had no children. All the girls I grew up with married and soon had families. I helped at the births of many of their children. We wondered why God had blessed us in every way but this. I did not feel God's presence withdrawn, only now I saw a different dimension. I had tried to fit God into my limited perception. Now I learned that God's ways are not always our ways. I felt the vastness of God and how little any of us can know. I learned

what it means to trust. I learned humility. And I learned compassion for all whose prayers seem to be unanswered. Years
went by, and we grew too old reasonably to expect to have
children. Zechariah gave up hope of having a son, but I clung
to the story of Sarah who was given a child when she was
ninety. Skeptical old Sarah laughed at God when she heard
she would have a son. And God laughed back at her. When
her son was born, he was named Isaac. which means "laughter." And I remembered Hannah, who in old age gave birth to
the great Samuel, whom she dedicated to God. I truly believe
that with God nothing is impossible. I continued to hope.

I poured out my love to the children in our village, and felt
a special bond with girls growing into womanhood. Next door
to us lived a lovely girl named Mary, who has been a lifelong
joy. Even after she married Clopas and moved to Emmaus,
she came back often, sharing her inner life as well as the out-
ward events, and always wanting to know what I was feeling
and thinking.

And God gave me another young girl to love, another daughter of my spirit. We have kinfolk in Galilee who stay with us
each year when they come to Jerusalem for the Passover. Their
little girl, also named Mary, was dear to me from the time she
was born. Even as a child she had a sense of God's presence, as
I had had, and this was a special bond. Year by year I watched
her grow in grace and beauty. She and the Mary next door were
the same age and became close friends, even though they saw
each other only once a year. They loved having the same name.

One year when the Galilee family came for the Passover,
Mary told us that she was betrothed. The man's name was
Joseph, and he was of the lineage of David the King. He was
some years older than Mary, a carpenter by trade, already well
established. Her parents had made a good choice for her,
though I sensed a bit of wistfulness in her. Was there someone closer in age who she had hoped might be her parents'
choice? I did not ask, and she did not say. She and Joseph
were to be married the next year.

Several months later it was time for Zechariah's division to be on duty as priests in the Temple. At such times they draw lots to determine who will burn incense on the altar of the Holy of Holies. Sometimes I went with Zechariah to Jerusalem and stayed with friends while he was on duty at the Temple, but this year I stayed home. I was tired.

Days went by, and it was time for him to return. I watched from the doorway and finally saw him in the distance. He looked tired and stooped and old. I felt concern. As he came into the house I was full of questions, but he shook his head and did not speak.

I washed his feet and brought clean clothes. He found the writing tablet and stylus and I watched as he traced letters. Soon I recognized the word and said it aloud, *Peni'el,* which means "the face of God." I quoted the passage from the Torah:

> So Jacob called the place Peniel, saying, "For I have seen God face to face, and yet my life is preserved." (Gen. 32:30)

I began to understand why he could not speak. It is a fearful thing to fall into the hands of the living God. (See Hebrews 10:31.)

I asked questions to which he could reply with a nod or shake of the head. Had the lot come to him to go to the altar? He nodded. Had something happened in the Holy of Holies? Again he nodded and then wrote the word *Gabriel.* After all his doubts about my angels he had finally encountered one himself! "Did Gabriel have a message?" I asked. In answer he touched my abdomen, making gestures rounding it to fullness. I gasped. "Are we really to have a child?" I asked. He nodded and drew me close, tears streaming down his face. Then he wrote, "His name will be John." A good name, I thought, for it means, "God is gracious." Zechariah let me know that he had questioned the prophecy, and Gabriel said he would lose the power of speech until the child is born.

After a simple supper we went to bed, he to sleep the sleep of exhaustion, and I to lie awake in wonder. After a time he roused and drew me close. God could not give us a child if we did not do our part. We made love with something of the passion of our early youth.

Some time passed before I was sure I would really have a child. I did not want to share our secret just yet, for our village is prone to gossip. I kept to the house and let Zechariah run the errands, even going for water each day. I'm sure there was much talk about his loss of speech.

By the time five months had gone by there was no hiding what had happened. The whole town buzzed with gossip, and there were jokes at Zechariah's expense. If people teased us, however, they did it lovingly. Our son became the child of the whole village, and everyone wanted to help. As the weeks went by, I wished my mother had lived to be with me now. I longed for family.

Then one day I looked out the doorway and could scarcely believe what I saw. My Mary from Nazareth was coming up the path, panting a little from the climb. I watched her come, and even before she reached our courtyard, I *knew*. I have seen too many young women with the bloom of early pregnancy on their limbs and the look of inward wonder on their faces not to recognize it in her. But how could this be? It was not yet time for her marriage to Joseph.

We embraced without words and I drew her into the house. I felt the child stir within me. She noticed and placed her hand tenderly on my swollen abdomen. Then in recognition of what I knew, I placed my hand on hers. She nodded. The tears, long held in, now came in torrents. We clung to each other and our tears mingled.

She said she had had a dream in which Gabriel came to her and said, "God is with you. Do not be afraid. You will have a son." In the dream she had asked, "How can this be? I'm not married yet." Gabriel responded that the child was holy, God's child, and Mary had finally answered, "Let it be according to your word."

Later, when she found that she really was pregnant, she was afraid. I was the person she felt could be counted on to understand and help. She found neighbors with whom she could make the long trip from Galilee to Judea. Now she turned her stricken face to me and asked, "Will anyone believe my story?" I held her close and said, "Mary, believe in your story. If you believe it, others will too."

Then once again I had a tremendous insight. Words of the prophet Isaiah came to me: "A voice cries out, 'In the wilderness prepare the way of the Sovereign, make straight in the desert a highway for our God'" (Isa. 40:3). And I knew that my son would be the voice in the wilderness, preparing the way for Mary's son. With humility I asked why this further miracle was given to me, that she should come to me now. I reached out and touched her, and though it was not yet time for her child to be moving, I felt the life in her.

Suddenly her doubts vanished and her face began to shine. She started to quote Hannah's song after she had given birth to Samuel. (See 1 Sam. 2:1–10.) Mary's own words mingled with Hannah's into something new, and the spirit of God was with her as she sang how her soul rejoiced in God who had regarded her low estate. (See Luke 1:47–48.)

Later I thought: Gabriel came to Zechariah. And Gabriel came to Mary. Might he not now come to Joseph in a dream, telling him to honor his betrothal? When I said this to Mary, she was doubtful, but I still felt it would happen.

Mary stayed until our son was born, and what help and strength and love she gave me. I had felt young again, being pregnant, but I was still an old woman and things became more difficult as the weeks wore on. Our child was not born without a struggle. How good to have Mary there to encourage me. She took care of the baby and kept the house going. I did not want to think of managing on my own, but I knew she must return home soon.

By the eighth day, when our John was to be circumcised, I felt stronger and able to cope with things. The neighbors gathered for the ceremony. They assumed our baby would be named for his father, and when I said his name was to be John, they protested. They turned to Zechariah, and he wrote on his tablet, "His name is John." Suddenly his speech returned. People fell silent, and his voice rang out with a great prayer of thanksgiving. Then he turned to address his small son, who looked up at him with solemn eyes:

> And you, child, will be called the prophet of the Most High . . .
> to give light to those who sit . . . in the shadow of death, to
> guide our feet into the way of peace. (Luke 1:76a, 79)

Zechariah lived only five more years. John and I have been alone as he has grown to maturity. He is tall, strong in body and in God's truth. As Gabriel foretold, he has something of the power and spirit of Elijah. Like me, he has always had a strong sense of God's presence. But he is also Zechariah's son and shares his devotion to the Torah. He lives by the law and imposes on himself arduous disciplines and fasts. I am concerned that he is judgmental of others. Most of us cannot live by the strict standards he sets for himself. I have heard him rebuke a man many years older for drunkenness, and a woman he saw glancing at a man not her husband. The village that welcomed him so warmly is now a little afraid of him. But they respect him and they listen to him, for he speaks with authority. He has his father's beautiful voice.

Most years we see Mary and Joseph and their family when they come for the Passover. The two young men, linked before birth, now present quite a contrast. John calls people to repent. He is full of *righteousness and truth*. Mary's son is more understanding of human weakness and need. He is gentle. He is full of *grace and truth*.

Soon John will be on his own. He hopes to go to the Essene community near Qumran for a time of study and preparation. He delays so that he may care for me. I do not want to be a burden to him. There is no fear in him. As he has rebuked the unrighteous in our little town, I know he will speak out against spiritual wickedness in high places. (See Ephesians 6:12.) I cannot help being afraid for him. He will be hurt and I will not be there to comfort him and care for him.

> O my God, You have never taken your Holy Spirit from me. You gave me grace to bear a child in my old age. Grant me now the grace to let go: to let go of my frail old body, and to let go of my son, trusting him to life. May he fulfill what his father prophesied for him at his birth: may he give light to those that sit in darkness. Let it be!

Comments

Another girl named Mary, later the wife of Clopas, has been introduced briefly into this story. She will tell her story in chapter 12. John's Gospel includes her in a group of women standing at the foot of the cross. It is an intimate group, for it includes Jesus' mother, her sister, and Mary Magdalene. But who is Mary, wife of Clopas? I think she must have been close to Mary the Mother, or she would not be part of this particular group. As I studied the map, I saw that Emmaus was probably in the hill country a little west of Jerusalem, although we are not sure of its location. I speculated that the two Marys might have known each other as girls through Elizabeth.

Elizabeth's was the first one of these stories that I wrote, perhaps because it was familiar to me in my childhood. Both my grandmothers had Elizabeth as a middle name, and I was given the name to honor them. One of them lived with us while I was growing up and instilled pride in the name by telling me stories of women named Elizabeth: Queen Elizabeth I of England, Saint Elizabeth of Hungary, Elizabeth Barrett Browning, Elizabeth Cady Stanton, Elizabeth Gurney Fry, and, of course, the biblical Elizabeth. I identified with each of the women, but felt especially close to Mary's kinswoman.

Traditionally we have thought of Elizabeth and Mary as cousins, but the difference in age makes kinswoman a better designation. Perhaps Elizabeth was Mary's aunt. The bond between them was obviously close, or Mary would not have made haste to set out on the long journey to visit her. And it was worth it. Elizabeth could give her the support she needed to face her unplanned pregnancy, by affirming that she was carrying a holy child. With that support Mary could face with courage and conviction her fiancé, her family, and her community, and could take her place in our religious tradition.

Reflections

1. We are told that Elizabeth and Zechariah were righteous. God obviously had blessed them in many ways. Yet they did not have children at the expected time. Have you experienced unanswered prayer? How did it affect your relationship with God? In the end, did something else happen? Was it better than what you had originally prayed for, or worse?

2. How do you feel about angels? What, if anything, leads you to believe they exist? What do you imagine an encounter with an angel might be like?

3. Was Zechariah's loss of speech divine punishment, or self-punishment? What leads you to this conclusion?

4. When you were young, did you confide in an older person not your parent? If so, what effect did this have on your relationship to that parent?

5. What gifts does age bring besides unexpected children?

6. Elizabeth spoke with authority about the future. Have you known people who were prophetic elders? Is this something acquired with age and experience? In what ways do we gain from—or miss out on—the wisdom of older people?

7. Both Matthew and Luke have genealogies of Jesus, tracing his lineage back to David through Joseph. Who do you think was the father of Jesus?

CHAPTER 2

Joanna

Luke 8:1–3, 23:55–56, 24:1–10; Matthew 2:16–18, 14:1–12

❧

For Herod had arrested John, bound him, and put him in prison on account of Herodias, his brother Philip's wife, because John had been telling him, "It is not lawful for you to have her."

—MATTHEW 14:3–4

Soon afterwards [Jesus] went on through cities and villages, proclaiming and bringing the good news. . . . The twelve were with him, as well as some women who had been cured of evil spirits and infirmities: Mary, called Magdalene, from whom seven demons had gone out, and Joanna, the wife of Herod's steward Chuza, and Susanna, and many others, who provided for them out of their resources.

—LUKE 8:1–3

Joanna's Story

I grew up in the palace in Jerusalem during the reign of Herod, known as "the Great." My father was one of his advisers and did much of the planning for Herod's large-scale building projects. The two of them changed the face of Judea. They built a splendid seaport on the Mediterranean and a number of strategically placed fortresses. They rebuilt the Temple in Jerusalem and constructed a magnificent palace beside it, connecting the two buildings with a viaduct. The people of Judea were initially pleased with Herod's reign, not only because of the Temple, but because he had married Mariamne, a Jew of the Maccabee family.

Herod was an Idumean, or Edomite. When Esau and Jacob separated, centuries ago, Edom became Esau's territory. Although he and Jacob were twins, their descendants have remained bitter enemies. Herod, the descendant of Esau, started his reign hoping to win the support of his subjects who call themselves "the children of Israel," the new name that Yahweh gave Jacob.

Even though Herod was put in power by the Romans and was himself subject to them, it is easy to see why he was called "the Great." He thought big, organizing and planning, surrounding himself with people capable of helping him realize his plans. Though he could be quite charming and was often generous, at times he was ruthless and brutal. My father never knew whether he would be working with a reasonable ruler who was appreciative of his adviser's abilities without being jealous of him, or a petty tyrant whom it was not safe to cross. He admired Herod's creative genius, but at times he feared for his life.

Herod was a law unto himself. He killed off those who were suspected of disloyalty without giving them a chance to explain or repent. In time he even killed his favorite wife, Mariamne, who was innocent of the charges against her. Any loyalty his subjects had felt for him was now gone.

As a girl, I saw only Herod's smiling face. He was fond of me and gave me beautiful gifts. I grew up in luxury, with many servants. I was an only child and much attention was lavished on me. When it was hot, someone fanned me; if it turned chilly, someone produced a warm wrap. I ate imported delicacies and always wore beautiful clothes. Anything I expressed a wish for was promptly supplied. Along with other palace children I learned to read and write and how to do simple figuring. My mother taught me to sew and to embroider. She was also concerned that I learn to deal firmly with servants and slaves, as befitted our status in the palace.

I often wanted to do things for myself and not have servants constantly hovering over me. As I grew into womanhood, I felt empty inside. There must be more to life than the pursuit of surface pleasures, I thought, but I did not know how or where to look for it. No one else seemed to question our extravagant way of life.

Soon after my twelfth birthday, I was married to Chuza, assistant to Herod's steward and in line to be a steward himself. The steward is a ruler's right-hand man, with oversight of his possessions, business affairs, property, and servants. In other words, he runs the palace. Chuza was good-looking, very capable, and ambitious. We were thought to be a good match.

Marriage was my only option, and this one would secure my future. No one, not even the two of us, asked if we loved each other. That was not why women of my class married. Within a few months we rejoiced that our first child was on the way. Chuza began trying out names for him. I secretly longed for a daughter.

Then something happened that changed everything. Herod received some visiting scholars, astronomers from Parthia, far to the east. They had seen a sign in the heavens that indicated a new ruler would be born in Judea. Herod, ever the gracious host, received them warmly. Privately he asked his priests to see what they could learn about this potential rival. They reported that the new king would be born in Bethlehem, a small town south of Jerusalem. Herod passed this word on to his guests, urging them to find the child, and then to return with news so that he might go himself to honor the new little ruler.

The astronomers departed for Bethlehem, but they did not return. Herod was angry and suspicious. He would not tolerate any threat to his rule. He impulsively sent a detachment of soldiers to Bethlehem with orders to kill every male child two years and younger—all the unweaned little boys. Surely the new rival to his power would be caught in this net.

I knew nothing of this until I heard some of the wives of the soldiers talking about it. The men were sickened by what they had done, snatching babies from their mothers' laps. They were afraid of Herod and had carried out his orders, but hated themselves for doing so.

I was shocked by what I heard, and became violently ill. That night I lost my child. I was afraid of Herod now. How could I go on living under the same roof with him? I prolonged my convalescence to avoid being with people and perhaps having contact with him. Chuza tried to comfort me, but he still had to work with Herod.

Before the next year was out, Herod died. His kingdom was divided among three of his sons. Philip was given the area in the north, east of the Sea of Galilee. Archelaus, his half brother, received the major southern territory, including Jerusalem. Antipas, now known as Herod Antipas, found himself with two territories not connected with one another: Galilee west of the Sea of Galilee in the north, and Peraea in the south, east of the Dead Sea. He now became known simply as Herod, but no one ever called him "the Great."

The new Herod asked Chuza to be his steward, and the two of them turned to the question of how to rule two widely separated territories. They decided that Herod must maintain palaces in both places, dividing his time between them.

Herod's father had built one of his fortresses, Machaerus, in Peraea. Herod remodeled it for his winter palace. That area is desert and unbearably hot in summer. Then the two of them planned a new city on the west bank of the Sea of Galilee. Herod called it Tiberias, to honor the Roman emperor. There he built a summer palace right on the shore. It is a joy to return each spring to the green hills of Galilee and to feel the cool breezes from the water throughout the hot season.

The long journey twice a year between the two palaces is quite an undertaking. The packing involves many days of work, and the journey itself often takes a week or more. Women and children travel in litters carried by slaves. The men ride horses or go in chariots.

We settled into the new life with the young Herod, and I lost my fear and depression. Chuza was close to him, and in his confidence, and Herod's wife and I became good friends. We hoped now for a child, but the months went by with no sign of one. Without children a woman seems unfulfilled. What could give meaning to my empty life?

Then someone important came into my life. I was given a new personal maid, named Mary, and before long I realized that she had the inner peace and joy for which I was longing. She has always served me faithfully, but with dignity, retaining her sense of self. In spite of my mother's teaching, I have never been harsh with her. I watch her go about her work, and I admire her efficiency and quickness. She gives each task her full attention. She never rushes, but does everything with grace, even joy. I longed to know her, to talk to her as an equal, but how could I bridge the gulf between us?

One year as we made the long journey south for the winter, we crossed the Jordan River at the ford just above the Dead Sea. When we reached the east side, we found a huge crowd spread out over the road. Our long procession came to a halt while soldiers cleared the way for us. I asked one of our bearers to find out what was going on in this rather barren place. He came back to report that a new prophet was preaching and baptizing on the bank of the Jordan.

Mary was sitting with me and I saw her face light up. I asked her what she knew, and she said that it must be John the Baptizer. Her brother had heard him preach, she said. He reported that John calls people to repent, then leads them into the water and baptizes them as a symbol of the new life they intend to lead. I realized that we were talking together, quite naturally. Was this the opportunity for friendship between us I had hoped for?

I asked if she would like to hear the prophet herself, and she nodded. I told her to go, and when she came back to the palace, I wanted to know everything that happened, and everything the prophet said. The next day she reported that John told people to repent because the reign of God is near at hand.

He said that those with two coats should give one to someone who had none, and those with food should share with the hungry. He told people not to use violence or make false accusations. (See Luke 3:10–14.)

Someone asked if John was the Messiah, the one to come, and John answered, "One who is more powerful than I is coming. I am not worthy to untie the thong of his sandals" (Luke 3:16). He quoted the prophet Isaiah, saying that he was "the voice of one crying out in the wilderness, 'Prepare the way of the Sovereign'" (Luke 3:4).

I asked Mary if she had been baptized. She nodded shyly. Her face was shining, and I envied her. I lay awake that night, thinking of all she had told me. The idea of sharing one's food and clothing was new to me. I'd never considered what it is like to be poor. I longed to go with Mary to hear John, but I was afraid. I tried to imagine what it would be like to be baptized and begin a new life of repentance and righteousness. From then on I thought of John day and night. The name Joanna is the feminine form of John, which means "God is gracious." This seemed a bond between the prophet and me.

Mary went back often to hear John preach. One day she reported that a tall young man joined the crowd. His face was so beautiful that she could not take her eyes from him. After John had baptized those who came forward, this man approached him. John shook his head, apparently reluctant to baptize him. Finally he consented, and the two of them went into the water. Mary said that after the baptism, the sun broke through the clouds, illuminating the young man's face. Then a dove lit on his head. People said this was a sign. Was this the one John had said would come? Mary learned that he is a kinsman of John from Nazareth in Galilee. His name is Jesus.

Life went on. Herod seemed more reasonable than his father, and Chuza enjoyed his confidence. Then, again, everything changed. Herod fell in love with his half brother Philip's wife. He put away his lawful wife, my good friend, and brought to the palace this ruthless, beautiful woman who assumed the name Herodias. Along with her came her spoiled daughter, Salome. They became part of the palace circle of women.

Utterly fearless and outspoken, John promptly denounced Herod for this sinful alliance. Herod had him arrested and put in the dungeon of the palace. I woke up that night realizing suddenly that the prophet and I were now under the same roof.

I bribed the guards to let me talk to him, paying them so well that no one knew I went daily to speak with John. There were bars between us, but I was truly "sitting at his feet," eager to learn all I could from him. He told me about his young kinsman, Jesus, who hopes to establish what he calls "the community of God," a new order of justice and peace. My life began to change. I dressed more simply and stopped wearing costly jewelry. I gave some to Mary to sell, so she could help people she knew who were in need.

Chuza was puzzled by the change in me, but he was glad I was happy. I did not tell him about my visits to John, knowing he would forbid them. I did ask what Herod intended to do with him. Chuza assured me that Herod would not kill John, fearing an uprising of the people if anything happened to him.

Herodias began planning a lavish party for Herod's birthday. She hired musicians and dancers and ordered elaborate food prepared. The palace buzzed with preparations and plans. Finally the evening arrived. The men gathered in the main banquet hall and the women in an adjoining room. I did not dare stay away, but I kept my distance from Herodias and Salome.

Late in the evening, after the hired entertainment was over, Herod sought some new way to amuse his guests. He sent to the women's hall to ask that Salome come and dance for the men. Herodias was reluctant, knowing the men were undoubtedly quite drunk by this time. Salome was eager, however, and Herod's messenger insistent.

The girl went to her quarters and changed into loose, quite transparent garments over which she draped veils of different

colors. She came back to the women's gathering briefly, so we
could all see her. Then she hurried after the servant.

After some time she returned. She told her mother that the
men had loved her dancing and had been wildly excited as she
took off veil after veil. Herod was delighted and promised on
his oath to give her anything she wanted. She did not know
what to ask for and wanted her mother's advice. Herodias
whispered something and Salome left the room. We went on
chatting while we nibbled on grapes and sweets.

The noise of the banquet hall quieted and we heard Herod
giving orders, but could not make out what he said. After a
long time Salome returned, wild-eyed and quite hysterical. She
carried to her mother a silver platter on which lay the head of
John, his eyes staring at us. I was not the only one who fainted.

The days drag on and there is no end to my grief for John.
Mary grieves with me. However, she keeps reminding me that
there is still Jesus. But where is he? How can we make contact with him? Mary listens to the news and gossip and soon
learns that he is returning to Galilee. I worry that Herod's
men may follow him and that he will not be safe on the road
north.

Chuza and I have talked about our future. He too was sickened by John's gruesome death. He understands that I can no
longer live at the palace. He will divorce me and then marry a
younger woman in whom he is interested. He wants children.
Since I have no brothers, I have inherited my father's estate. I
can take care of myself.

John had told me that the community Jesus wants to establish is for the poor and oppressed, for peacemakers, and those
who are pure of heart. And it is for those who hunger and
thirst for righteousness. He said that those who mourn will
find comfort. I asked John if it is for women too. He nodded,
adding that it is for children also. It is for everyone who truly
seeks it, he said.

Mary already has that purity of heart. We are friends now,
planning our future together. She makes me think I can really

lead a new life and can adjust to the hardships involved. With her help and love I feel confident I can learn to live more simply.

John had said he was "a voice crying in the wilderness." Here in the wilderness of Peraea, I can see in my mind's eye the highway he worked to prepare for Jesus. For me now the desert is no longer a wasteland. There are springs of living water for the thirsty. John told me that God cares about the small sparrows that fall to the ground and that God loves the bright flowers that last only a few days. The desert, indeed the whole earth now, shines for me with the presence of God.

It is nearly time for our annual move north with the spring. My heart is already in Galilee, for that is where Jesus is. We will find him. I have hungered and thirsted for righteousness for so long. Surely Jesus will not turn me away. Surely the community of God is for me, too.

Comments

Over the years I have read the brief reference to Joanna in Luke's eighth chapter and wondered what a woman of the palace was doing tramping the dusty roads of Galilee with an itinerant rabbi and a bunch of fishermen. Then I remembered the two bloody incidents: the murder of the little boys of Bethlehem by Herod the Great, and the death of John the Baptist at the hands of Herod Antipas, his son. These were reasons enough for a sensitive person to want to leave the palace life.

It seemed logical to have this chapter follow Elizabeth's, to continue the story of John the Baptist, even though this places Joanna's story earlier than the biblical references to her. Because her story comes so early, we cannot complete it here. Women in later chapters will refer to her so the reader will know what happens after she and Mary reach Galilee and find Jesus. (You should know that Luke, in 24:1, tells us she was with Jesus till the end.)

Joanna was probably better educated than any of the other women around Jesus and had been close to the center of power in her life at the palace. I have let her explain the historical situation and the geography, rather than writing about them here.

Since Luke indicates that Joanna was one of those who "provided for Jesus and his male disciples out of their means," I have made her an only child. If there were no brothers, a woman could inherit from her father. Incidentally, the word "provided for" in the Greek is *diakineo,* which means "to serve, as a deacon." This suggests that Joanna and the other women who traveled with Jesus were not in a servant role, but an equal, vital part of the group. If they were servants, it may be in the sense that Jesus meant when he said "the one who is great must be the servant of all" (Matt. 20:26–27).

There appears to have been no scandal in their traveling together, this mixed group of men and women. As scholars point out, the Gospel writers wanted to convince people that Jesus was the Messiah. There seems to be no reason to include the women except that they are so important they could not be left out completely. Luke plays down their importance by saying they "had been cured of evil spirits and infirmities." He names three and adds that there were "many others." Since he mentions twelve men, one gets the impression that the women must have outnumbered them.

Luke also mentions Susanna, but gives no clue as to who she was, so there was nothing on which I could build a story. I am sorry, for she must have been important to be mentioned by name and not lumped with the "many others."

As I lived with Joanna, seeking to evoke her story, I felt that it would have been difficult to make this drastic change without some help. One day as I was thinking of her, she quite simply let me know that there was someone, and a servant at that. In time, Mary, her personal maid, came to seem as real to me as Joanna herself.

"To sit at the feet of " means to study with, as Paul got his legal training by "sitting at the feet of Gamaliel" (Acts 22:3). Since Joanna had more education than most of the followers of Jesus, I felt she would use her opportunity to be with John in the dungeon to learn all that she could.

Reflections

1. What, if anything, leads you to think that John the Baptist was sent to pave the way for Jesus? What would prompt the need for Jesus' way to be prepared?

2. Given all the women whose stories have not been included in the New Testament, what would prompt including the sordid story of Salome's dance and its tragic aftermath? What is it about this story that continues to titillate us right down to the twentieth century? (For example, Richard Strauss's opera *Salome.*)

3. Joanna had to simplify her life drastically in joining Jesus. Have you ever tried to make such a change? What did you learn from the experience?

4. Early English translators of the Bible lived in a monarchy, so the phrase "the kingdom of God" seemed natural to them. Some of us live in democracies. How do you react to the word "kingdom"? Does "community of God" seem an appropriate substitute?

5. Can we hope for a worldwide community of justice and peace, or must it be only within us, as Jesus suggested? Have you been part of an intentional community based on such ideals? Did the community live up to its original vision? What happened?

6. Pope John XXIII at the Second Vatican Council in 1962 called on the church to "make a preferential option for the poor." What do you think of "liberation theology"? Do you believe the hierarchy of the Roman Catholic Church should support it today?

CHAPTER 3

The Woman at the Well

John 4:1–42

❧

[Jesus] left Judea and started back to Galilee. But he had to go through Samaria. So he came to a Samaritan city called Sychar, near the plot of ground that Jacob had given to his son Joseph. Jacob's well was there, and Jesus, tired out by the journey, was sitting by the well. It was about noon. A Samaritan woman came to draw water, and Jesus said to her, "Give me a drink."

—JOHN 4:3–7

The Story of the Woman at the Well

To begin with, I have three counts against me. First, I am a woman, and to be born a woman is to have abilities you cannot use and dreams you cannot fulfill. It is to be vulnerable, to have little control over your life, even over your own body. It is to hunger for something—or someone—and never to be satisfied.

Second, I am a Samaritan, a member of a small, despised group surrounded by people who feel innately superior. And that is strange, for we and the Jews all look back to Sarah and Abraham, to Rebekah and Isaac, to Leah and Rachel and Jacob. We worship the One God, although in different places.

Third, there is my reputation. It does sound rather bad: five husbands, and then living with a man to whom I am not married. A woman is never allowed to forget her past, no matter how sincere her repentance and blameless her new life. Rahab will always be Rahab the harlot, and I will always be the anonymous woman who went through five husbands.

So let me tell you my story. I have lived all my life in the village of Sychar. Like most towns, it is built around a well, the gathering place for news and gossip. However, a little distance from town is another well, very ancient and of great depth, with cold, pure water. It is harder to draw from so deep a well, so few people in town use it. It is called Jacob's well, because it is said to have been found by Jacob and Rachel and shared with their son Joseph.

My father was a successful shepherd. He watered his flocks at Jacob's well and we got our household water there because it tastes better. I continue to use the well. I like to go there around noon when there is seldom anyone about. It is my time to be alone, and I need that time. It has been important in my struggle to survive with a sense of myself.

And I've hung on to my sense of humor too. I was bright and quick as a child and early learned to say clever things. My father would scold, but I saw his suppressed laughter. I grew up to be outspoken, and no one—not my father, nor any of my husbands—could break me of it, although they all tried. Too often my outspoken words turned out to be right. I gained a reputation for being able to read the signs of the times and earned a certain respect in the town, in spite of all the husbands.

When I was growing up, we lived near a family with a boy about my age whose name was Jacob. His father was a shepherd, like mine, and we both helped our fathers watch the sheep. Childhood friendship and companionship grew into adolescent love. We hoped our fathers would arrange a marriage.

Then the two men had a bitter quarrel over some missing sheep. Suddenly we were forbidden to see each other. We met at the well a few times, but were caught and punished.

My father began to seek a suitable husband for me. One day he simply announced that arrangements were complete. My protests resulted in a beating, and the marriage took place soon after.

My husband was the eldest of five brothers. He had been married before, but had no children. He was well-to-do, which was what made him a good match in my father's eyes, but he was already advanced in age and needed a caretaker more than a wife. There would be no sons from this marriage. It was a relief when he died a few years later. I hoped I might marry Jacob now.

My father reminded me that according to custom, I must be married to one of my husband's brothers, in hope for a son to carry on the first husband's name. He approached another brother, and my second marriage was arranged. This man already had sons by another marriage and had little interest in giving his deceased brother a child. He felt he had done me a favor by marrying me and was entitled to my services. There was no pleasing him. He finally divorced me and turned me out of the house.

My father went to the third brother. This man was kinder and wanted children, but none were born to us. Was it my fault? No one ever blames the man. He insisted I must be barren, and made plans to marry someone else.

The fourth brother was nearer my age, but there was no love between us. He taunted me with the large dowry my father had paid to get rid of me. He called me shopworn, and most nights he ignored me. He divorced me to marry a younger woman.

By now I was past caring. Jacob was married to someone else. I was no longer young, and before long I would be past the childbearing age, with not even one child to justify my unhappy existence. Once again my father paid a high dowry and married me to the last brother. He was younger than I and, if possible, less compatible with me than his brothers. He was a merchant, gone from home for months at a time.

Finally one of his trips stretched on for months with no word from him. Eventually another merchant brought word that he had been killed in a drunken brawl. I was free at last. His house and assets came to me. My mother had died and my father was unwell. I moved in to care for him for the last months of his life. Then my childhood home also came to me. Suddenly, from having nothing I was a woman of property and substance.

Meanwhile, Jacob's marriage had been a stable one. His wife was a good woman and they had several children, all grown now. Jacob was a grandfather! His wife had become paralyzed and lay on her pallet day after day, unable to move or speak. Jacob hired a woman to care for her. He had inherited his father's flocks and prospered.

For a time we hoped death would release her quickly and free us to marry and spend our last years together. But she lingered on and Jacob did not feel free to divorce her. I couldn't see that it would make any difference. He could still pay for her care. I loved Jacob too much to insist on marriage.

We were mature adults. Everyone knew of our love for each other. There were no longer parents to interfere; we could be open now. We began to share meals at my house and to make a life together. In time it was only natural to share the same bed. There was no possibility of a child now. So, after five unhappy marriages, I learned the fulfillment of married love from a man not free to marry me. We were happy. Yet still I always had an inner thirst for something more to give my life meaning.

One day about noon, as I approached Jacob's well, I saw from a distance a man sitting on the curbing. It was not Jacob. As I came closer I could tell from his dress that he was a Jew, and I resented his presence. What was he doing in Samaria? Why had he stopped at *my* well? As I came up I saw that he was tired. He said urgently, "Give me a drink."

Now, Jews are strictly forbidden to eat or drink from the same vessels as Samaritans. Moreover, men should not speak

to women they do not know in public places. In my usual outspoken fashion I blurted out, "You are a Jew and I am a Samaritan, so how can you ask me for a drink?" He laughed and
said that he realized that if the situation were reversed, and I
were in Judea asking for a drink, I would not get it. I laughed
and let down my pitcher. When I drew it up, I tipped it for him
to drink and he sighed with pleasure. In spite of myself, I liked
him. We sat there companionably, and then he said, "If only
you recognized God's gift, and who it is that is asking you for a
drink, you would have asked him for a drink instead, and he
would have given you living water."

I felt defensive. Our well does not give stale water like the
water you get from a cistern. "Sir," I said, "you have no bucket
with which to draw water and this well is very deep. Where
would you get living water? Are you greater than our ancestors, Rachel and Jacob, who gave us this well and drank from
it themselves?"

Seeing my confusion, he responded, "If you drink from this
well you will soon be thirsty again, but if you drink the water I
can give you, you will be satisfied. That water will be like a
spring inside you, eternally welling up." How did he know my
inner thirst? "Sir," I said, "I beg you, give me this living water
that I may thirst no longer."

And then he had to spoil it. I could not believe what I heard
next. He said, "Go call your husband and come back." I was
disappointed and confused. I was a person in my own right, not
an adjunct to a husband! I said quietly, "I have no husband."
"Well," he responded, "you are honest. You've had five husbands
and are not married to the man with whom you are living."

I looked at him in astonishment. How could this stranger
know my story? I realized that this was no ordinary man. Could
he be the long-awaited Messiah? I decided to test him. If he
was *the one to come,* he must be for everyone, not just for the
Jews. Very respectfully I said, "Sir, I see you are a prophet. My
people believe that Mount Gerazim is the place to worship
God, and you have your temple in Jerusalem. Why have you
come here?"

"Believe me," he said, "the time is coming when you will worship God neither on Mount Gerazim nor in Jerusalem. The time is coming, in fact it is already here, when those who worship truly will worship in spirit and truth. God seeks such worshipers." I thought about this and said quietly, "I know that the Messiah is coming and then all these things will be revealed." I stopped. I turned to look at him. And then I *knew*.

Before I could drop to my knees before him, we heard voices. Now it appeared that he had companions who had gone into town to buy food. They seemed upset when they saw him talking to a Samaritan woman. Knowing that they must also be thirsty, I left my pitcher for them, and returned to my home.

My head was whirling. It simply was not possible that the Messiah would come to me, a woman, one of doubtful reputation, and a Samaritan! And yet, I believed him. He had understood my inner thirst and had offered me living water to satisfy it. As I came into town, people saw my excitement. Someone asked, "What's happened?" I answered, "I have just met a man at Jacob's well who knew all about me. I think he might be the Messiah."

People crowded around and I told them all that had happened. They asked if I thought he was still at Jacob's well, and I nodded. I led the way and brought them all to Jesus.

He welcomed them and at my urging explained about worshiping in spirit and in truth. They listened, asked questions, and were satisfied with his answers. Finally Jacob said, "Rabbi, stay with us and teach us more." He talked to his friends and they agreed to stay two more days. Now people came and thanked me. "He was all that you said he was, and more," someone said. And another added, "We were ready to believe he might be the Messiah from what you said, but now we have heard for ourselves."

It was getting late. We agreed to go to our homes and to gather in a little while at the town well, bringing food to share. Soon we laid our bread, dried fish, and fruit from our trees before him. He blessed the food and broke the bread. We passed the food around and no one went hungry. He told us his name was Joshua in the Hebrew tongue, or Jesus in the Greek. He introduced us to his friends, Andrew and his brother Simon, and Philip and Nathaniel. (See John 1:35–51.) We all told him our names, and during the days he was with us he called us all by name.

Then he talked about the *community of God*. It is not like the Roman Empire where so-called important people lord it over others. In God's community the poor, the sick, the heavily burdened, the oppressed are all important. It is for women and children, he said, as well as men. It is for sinners, for God loves and forgives us. Someone broke in and asked, "Yes, but for Samaritans too?" "Yes," he answered, "for everyone."

"Do not think of yourselves as servants or slaves, or subjects of a ruler who is remote and whose intentions you do not understand," he told us. "In a community we are all friends. I have called you friends," he went on, "because I have made known to you everything that I have heard from my Father" (John 15:15).

He told us we need not wait for someone to drive out the Romans, or make peace between Jews and Samaritans. "The community of God is already here," he said. "It is within us, like a fountain of living water. We live in it now, where we are." People listened intently, trying to understand.

He had a beautiful voice and from time to time he quoted from the prophets. I remember this passage from Jeremiah:

[Thus] saith our God: My people have committed two evils: they have forsaken me, the fountain of living water, and dug out cisterns for themselves, cracked cisterns that can hold no water. (Jer. 2:13)

and this from Isaiah:

Ho, everyone who thirsts, come to the waters;
and you that have no money, come, buy and eat!
Come, buy wine and milk without money and without price.

Why do you spend money for that which is not bread,
And your labor for that which does not satisfy?

—ISAIAH 55:1–2b

When he had finished, we all sat quietly, thinking about what he had said. Then he said, "Go, sleep in peace, and we will gather again tomorrow evening."

The next day Jacob and I asked if we might talk to him. The three of us walked to the well and sat down on the rim. We poured out our story, holding nothing back. He looked at us quietly and said, "Those who love much are forgiven much." (See Luke 7:47.) Jacob and I looked at each other and knew we must leave our broken cistern for the fountain of living water.

I realized I no longer wished Jacob's wife dead. My heart went out to her in pity. When we walked back to town, we went to Jacob's house. Jesus stood by the mat where Jacob's wife lay immobile. He told her that she was God's daughter and that it was not God's will for her to lie there unable to move. With an effort she slowly turned her head toward him and her frozen face began to smile. He took her by the hand and gently helped her rise. She seemed like her old self. Jacob went to her and gathered her into his arms.

For just a moment I thought my heart would break. Then I looked at Jesus and felt living water deep within me. I will always love Jacob, but I no longer need to possess him. I can let him go.

When we gathered in the evening, Jacob's wife was there with him. News of her healing had spread rapidly through the town, and people had brought their loved ones, the blind grandmothers, the crippled children, and those possessed by demons. One by one Jesus healed them. He talked about what it means to be whole, and told us he had come that we might have life in all its fullness.

In the morning, Jesus asked if he and I might walk to the well one last time. His friends would join him later and they would go on to Galilee. He said they were good men and in time they would be powerful teachers, but that sometimes they were slow to understand. He said, "But you understood right away, and you brought the whole town to me." He asked if I would be his messenger to Samaria. I knelt and he blessed me and we prayed that I might be a clear channel for the living water.

So I will climb the mountains of my country, going to the smallest villages. I will follow narrow tracks to isolated homes, to bring the good news of the community of God. My message will be for everyone, but especially for women, for I know their thirst, and I know that water from broken cisterns cannot satisfy it.

And to everyone I will tell how the Messiah came to me, a weary traveler, wearing the clothes of the enemy, and asking for a drink of water.

Comments

After the death of John the Baptist, Jesus decides to return to Galilee to begin his ministry there. He knows Herod's men are watching him, so he does not go by the main road along the Jordan River, where he would be conspicuous and vulnerable, but takes the inner mountainous route through Samaria.

Samaria needs a bit of historical background. In his forty-year reign (1010–970 B.C.E.), David consolidated the whole area we know as Palestine into one kingdom. His son Solomon followed him. For all his reputed wisdom, Solomon left the kingdom weak and impoverished. At his death in 922 B.C.E., the kingdom was split into two small nations: Judah in the south, and Israel in the north. Samaria was part of the northern kingdom; the city of Samaria its capital. Israel was conquered by the Assyrians in 721 B.C.E. and Judah by the Babylonians in 587 B.C.E. Large numbers of both groups were carried off into slavery.

After the exile people returned, about 520 B.C.E. The bitter hatred between Jews and Samaritans goes back to that time. Nehemiah, the leading figure in the return, believed in racial purity. It was only natural that there had been intermarriage by Jews with Assyrians and Babylonians during the exile. Nehemiah insisted Jewish men must divorce their "foreign" wives, a devastating order, for most had children.

Samaritans offered to help rebuild the Temple in Jerusalem, but Nehemiah turned them down. He claimed they were descendants of non-Jewish colonists from Assyria who had settled there after the Israelites were deported. Samaritans themselves claim to go back to the time of Judges in Israel and base their lives on the Torah. Forbidden to worship at the Temple in Jerusalem, they built their own temple on Mount Gerazim, not far from the site of the well in our story. Descendants of the Samaritans still live in the area, in the modern city of Nablus.

At the time of Jesus, "Samaritan" was an epithet implying someone of inferior and dubious background. Jesus forever changed the meaning of the word with his story of the good Samaritan.

John's story is long. I have followed it quite closely. John often writes with great vividness and detail, like an eyewitness. One can almost believe the Gospel was written by John the disciple, although most scholars place it later.

My main problem in creating the story was explaining the acceptance by the townspeople of a woman of such dubious reputation. They seem to respect her and trust her reading of things. They all went with her to meet Jesus. The custom of levirate marriages could reasonably explain the five husbands. And the town was small enough that everyone probably knew she had loved someone for many years but was not free to marry him. Having property would probably enhance her status.

As for Jesus knowing things about people that he has not been told, I sometimes find that I have intuitive knowledge of people on first meeting, and sometimes I have been known in such a way by others. I'll admit that getting the actual number of marriages right seems too much coincidence. But after all, five has always been a magic number, one people would use in telling a story, whether it exactly fit the facts or not.

Reflections

1. Comment on the importance of the well in people's lives in both Old and New Testaments. What equivalent, if any, do we have in our communities today?

2. Why would people in Sychar believe the word of a woman who has had five husbands and is now living with someone to whom she is not married?

3. Have you ever had intuitive knowledge of someone on first meeting? Did this knowledge later prove to be accurate? How did it affect your relationship with that person?

4. Does love for someone involve letting that person go, if it is necessary for that person's growth and self-fulfillment? It is probably necessary for parents to let children go, but it is also true of partners or spouses?

5. Prejudice against Samaritans was prevalent in Jesus' time. Prejudice and racism are still with us after two thousand years. Do you think they are inherent in human society?

6. This story in John is at the beginning of Jesus' ministry. We find him sharing his message with Samaritans. Later he told the Syrophoenician woman (see chapter 6) that he was sent only to his own people. What might Jesus have meant by this apparent inconsistency? Who are Jesus' own people?

CHAPTER 4

Simon Peter's Mother-in-Law

Matthew 4:12–13, 18–22; Mark 1:14–34;
John 1:35–51, 21:1–13

❧

Now when Jesus heard that John had been arrested, he withdrew to Galilee. He left Nazareth and made his home in Capernaum by the sea.

—MATTHEW 4:12–13

When the sabbath came, he entered the synagogue and taught. They were astounded at his teaching, for he taught them as one having authority and not as the scribes.

—MARK 1:21b–22

As soon as they left the synagogue, they entered the house of Simon and Andrew, with James and John. Now Simon's mother-in-law was in bed with a fever, and they told him about her at once. He came and took her by the hand and lifted her up. The fever left her, and she began to serve them.

—MARK 1:29–31

The Story of Simon Peter's Mother-in-Law

My husband came home after a night of fishing and announced during breakfast that he had arranged a marriage for our daughter. I caught my breath and sighed. She was only twelve, small for her age, delicate. She never had been robust. I had hoped for more time before she left home to take on all the responsibilities of marriage. My husband saw my hesitation. He was very tired and responded irritably, "Well, she's twelve now. She's a woman. I did not want to pass up a good prospect for her."

I asked if the man was a fisherman. He nodded. How could I tell him that I had hoped for an easier life than mine for our daughter? He had always worked hard, and we never lacked for food, but fishing does not allow a normal family life. The men go out to fish in the evening when the wind dies down. If the fishing is good, they fish all night. When it begins to get light, they sell their catches to the fish dealers, mend their nets, and come home for breakfast. They sleep most of the day. The children must be kept quiet lest they wake their father. Also it is hard to be alone at night with the children. I never slept well for worrying about our safety at home and his on the water. Sudden storms come up; boats capsize, and men sometimes drown. I wanted a more normal life for our daughter.

Just then she came in and heard the news. Eagerly she asked, "What's he like?" Her father told her his name is Simon and that he and his brother Andrew have a good boat. They come from Bethsaida, the town just east of Capernaum, where we live. He said that Simon is honest, hardworking, and good-hearted. He and his brother have done well. "But what does he look like?" she asked. Her father shrugged. "Dark, curly hair. Stocky. He may seem a bit rough to you at first, but he's a good man." She asked, "If I don't like him, do I have to go through with it?" He told her it was all settled and there was no backing out.

He had talked with Simon that morning while they mended nets. Simon said that his family home was overcrowded with his older brothers and their families. He felt it was time to have a home of his own. He had found a little house on the main street of Capernaum, and all he needed was a wife. My husband asked about the bride price. It had been a very good night and Simon said that whatever the fish dealer paid my husband for his night's catch would be satisfactory. And so it was settled. Simon planned to fix up the house. He hoped to be married in a few months.

There was nothing to do but accept it. My daughter and I set to work to make the linen she would need for her new home. Our days were full spinning, weaving, and sewing. I was satisfied that she could do all these things well. We made her new clothes: a beautiful tunic for the wedding and plainer ones for ordinary days. We also made swaddling clothes, for of course there would soon be children.

Each day when we went to the well for water we passed the house. It seemed small to her. I pointed out that it was about as big as the other houses in town. As the weeks went by, Simon put in partitions, made cupboards and repaired the window frames and door. The house would be snug and waterproof, as well as convenient. She grew excited.

As I came to know Simon, I found that he is indeed honest and hardworking. He means well. Even so, I found him a bit rough and impetuous, given to speaking his mind hastily and then making a clumsy apology. I was more disturbed to find that he is a radical. He talks openly about a revolt against the Romans. It is time for the Messiah to come, he said, to drive out the hated legions that occupy our little country. I worried that he would join a revolution and when it was put down might be crucified as a traitor. Not a happy prospect for our daughter. She laughed at my fears. She looked forward to being married.

On the appointed day we walked the short distance to Simon's house and found most of the town gathered already. A feast had been prepared and people were eating and drinking. Simon saw us and rushed up. He took his bride by the hand. People formed a circle around them, singing and clapping as they danced. She looked lovely in her new clothes, and she danced with liveliness and grace. Simon was delighted with her and kept telling everyone how lucky he was to have such a beautiful young bride.

Late in the evening Simon encouraged people to go home, but the guests only teased him and made rude jokes while they drank his wine. What a way for a young girl to begin her marriage, I thought. Then I remembered that that was just the way my own marriage had started.

As expected, our daughter was soon pregnant. The smell of food nauseated her, and many days she did not get out of bed. I went over each day to help. At first Simon was concerned and sympathetic, but when it went on for weeks, he grew impatient. He went out fishing whether he felt well or not. Why couldn't she work when her stomach was upset? I tried to reason with him, but he would not listen. The more he scolded the worse she felt. I continued to come over each day to keep things going.

Then one morning my husband staggered in before it began to be light. He was very ill. I got him to bed and bathed him with cold cloths. When I touched him I found that he was burning up with fever. His throat hurt and he was having trouble swallowing. I made chicken broth, but he would not take more than a few sips. He was no better the next day, and then red sores came out over much of his body. The midwife healer came, looked at him, and said he should drink more, but I saw she really didn't think there was much hope. He died a few weeks before his grandson was born. We gave him a proper burial and I mourned him sincerely. He had always treated me well.

Our daughter had a hard birth, as often happens with a first child. I worked with the midwife to get her through the ordeal, but she was slow to recover. The baby, however, was healthy and quite beautiful. I still came over each day to take care of him as well as to cook for the family and keep the house clean.

Simon suggested that I give up my house and move in with them. It made sense. My house seemed empty without my husband. Soon there was a second child, a little girl. This delivery was easier, but again the mother had no energy for anything but to nurse her. I was finding that my strength was not what it was when I was young and having babies of my own. I went to bed each night bone-tired, hoping the baby would let me sleep, but even if the house was quiet, I often lay awake and worried. What if something happened to Simon? What if I became ill and could not work? What would become of our daughter and her small children if she never got her strength back?

As time went on I came to know the people in the house next door. The man's name is Zebedee. He is prosperous and owns several fishing boats. His sons, James and John, work with him. They and Simon and Andrew are good friends. Zebedee's wife is good-hearted. She comes over often and if she sees something that needs doing, she just does it without fuss. She loves to talk and gossip. Nothing goes on in town but what she knows about it.

One day she asked if Simon had said anything about going to Judea. I looked at her in astonishment and shook my head. She said her boys had told her that there was a new prophet preaching near the ford of the Jordan River, just above the Dead Sea. He called people to repent, because he said that the reign of God is at hand. Her sons said that Simon and Andrew wanted to see if this was the Messiah. Zebedee had talked their sons out of going. I was upset. How would we manage with Simon gone? She said that as long as her men could fish, there would be food for us too.

When Andrew came home with Simon I confronted them. They admitted they planned to go Judea soon to see this new prophet in person. The fishing was going well. Simon would lay in supplies and leave enough money to run the house for some time. I tried to talk them out of this wild journey, but Simon said that if this really was the Messiah, he wanted to join the movement in the beginning. I did not find that reassuring.

A few days later they left. For weeks there was no word. I tried not to worry, for I needed my sleep, but most nights I didn't get much rest. In the morning my good-hearted neighbor would talk me out of the worst of my fears. But then, she still had her husband, and her sons had not gone off after some self-styled Messiah.

Then one morning they returned, exhausted and discouraged. The prophet had been arrested and finally put to death. I washed their feet and fed them and they slept. In the evening they went fishing and life settled down again. Simon was tender with his wife and delighted to see how his children had grown. He seemed so happy I hoped this was the end of his revolutionary foolishness. Soon there was another child on the way.

My neighbor continued to come each day, helping as usual and letting me know what was going on in town. One day she reported that a stranger had moved into a little house on the edge of town. Word was that he was a rabbi who had been run out of his hometown to the south. Why has he come here? I asked. She did not know. I wondered why Simon had not mentioned this new rabbi. I had a premonition of trouble.

In the morning I got breakfast ready, but Simon did not come home. Time dragged on. Hoping for news of our men, I went next door to see if Zebedee and his sons had returned. Zebedee had just come in, exhausted and upset. His wife had a hard time getting anything coherent out of him. Finally we pieced together what had happened. Zebedee and his sons were sitting in the boat, mending their nets, when a man came walking along the shore. Zebedee guessed he was the new rabbi who had come to town. The man said to James and John, "Follow me, and I will teach you to fish for people." The boys climbed right out of the boat, leaving their father sitting there. Simon and Andrew joined them and he thought they had all gone into town. Zebedee's wife was outraged. "They can't do this to us," she stormed. "Zebedee must go at once and find them." But he was too tired and already asleep. I went back home and told my daughter all that had happened.

Late in the evening Simon came home. He said that the man was a kinsman of the prophet John, whom they had met in Judea. John intimated that this man is the Messiah. His name is Jesus. They had actually walked back to Galilee with him, parting from him where the road branches off for Nazareth, his hometown. Things had not gone well for him there and he decided to make his headquarters in Capernaum. He would be teaching and preaching in Galilee. The four young men were his first followers. He said they would not be far from home and would come back to Capernaum frequently. It would be their home base.

When I told him what Zebedee had said, Simon filled in the details. The fishing had not been good. Toward dawn Zebedee and his sons gave up and rowed into shore to mend the nets. He and Andrew decided to stay out a bit longer. They heard someone call. Voices carry well over water. On the shore they saw a man who had a fire going. He called out to ask if they had any fish. Simon said they had fished all night and taken nothing.

The man told them to cast their net on the other side of the boat. Simon thought it useless, but finally tried it. At once the net was so full that it was a struggle to manage it. James and John came over to help. The man on the shore was Jesus. He had made bread and now roasted some of the fish, and they all had breakfast.

James and John took bread and fish to their father and got back in the boat with him. Simon negotiated with the fish dealer, while Andrew helped Jesus clean up and put out the fire. Jesus asked them to be his disciples and they agreed. The three walked to Zebedee's boat, and Jesus asked James and John to follow him also. They had all gone with him to the little house where Jesus lives. He outlined his plans to teach and preach in Galilee.

I was upset by this tale and could not sleep that night. In the morning my throat was sore. When I tried to get up, I realized I had a high fever. I remembered my husband's final illness. I told my daughter she would have to do without me, and she dutifully got up and set about preparing breakfast.

At sundown the Sabbath began. We heard that Jesus would preach in our synagogue in the morning. My neighbor told me about it later. Everyone in town came and the synagogue was filled. Presently Jesus entered with the four young men. He talked for some time, she said; she added that he had a beautiful voice. She was in the women's section at the back and had trouble following what he said. Afterwards people said he spoke with authority, not like the scribes who usually speak. Then a man with a demon stood up and shouted at him. Jesus rebuked the demon and the man fell down limp. Jesus helped him rise. People saw that he was in his right mind again. They were astonished that Jesus had authority over demons. I listened and turned restlessly on my pallet. She brought me a drink of water.

Now we heard what sounded like a crowd of people coming down the street. My daughter went to the door to see what was happening. Before she could say anything we heard Simon say, "Rabbi, my mother-in-law has a high fever. Can you help her?" I wanted to hide, but there is no hiding place in this little house.

And then Jesus was there, standing by my pallet. He was not as I had imagined. He was gentle, yet with great strength. His presence filled the room. He took my hand, and I felt an incredible surge of power go through me. For a moment I was afraid, but then a great sense of well-being filled me. I realized my fever was gone and my throat no longer hurt. Gently he helped me to my feet. I did not feel like an old woman with failing strength. I was a person who could do whatever was needed.

I looked around at a house full of people. I went to the kitchen and made bread. We always have fish to feed a multitude. Soon I was passing out bread and fish and wine to everyone. People said it tasted like a wedding feast. I worked without strain, with joy really. When you make bread with joy, it tastes better, I thought.

Word of my healing spread through town. Now people brought loved ones who were sick or possessed of demons and gathered in the street outside our house. Jesus stood in the doorway and healed them, one by one. He began to speak and his voice carried. I remember that he said:

> Do not worry about your life, what you will eat or what you will drink . . . or what you will wear. Is not life more than food, and the body more than clothing? . . . Look at the birds of the air; they neither sow nor reap nor gather into barns, and yet [God] feeds them. Are you not of more value than they? (Matt. 6:25–26)

Sundown came and people left quietly. I know there was joy in many homes that night. Jesus came back into our house. He turned to my daughter, lying there with her baby and asked her, "Would you really like to be whole?" I saw her look at him and take in the tremendous wholeness of Jesus. Without hesitation she said, "Yes, I want to be whole." He took her by the hand and helped her to her feet. She was changed. I watched her take charge with confidence. She said to me, "Mother, you rest. I'll clear up the dishes and put the food away."

Jesus blessed all of us, including the children, calling us each by name. When he came to Simon, he called him Simon Peter. He said that Simon means "one who listens," and Simon had listened to his message. And Peter means "rock." He would be the solid foundation of the new movement. I saw Peter stand a little taller.

Andrew walked back with Jesus to the little house, but Simon Peter spent the night with his family. I told him I had no more reservations. I did not think that Jesus would drive out the Romans, but I was certain that the power of God is in him. I told him to feel free to follow Jesus wherever he might go.

Peter put his arm around me and said, "I am a lucky man. I have found the Messiah and given my life to him. I have a beautiful wife and children. And, I have *you* for a mother-in-law!"

Comments

The locale of this story is very vivid to me. In 1982 my husband and I visited Israel. After some time in Judea, we turned northward to Galilee. Jerusalem, Bethlehem, and Nazareth are all modern cities, but when we came to Capernaum, we found an archeological dig. Until 1894 the place was covered with shrubby plants and thistles, and a Bedouin tribe eked out a poor existence there.

Then a Franciscan order bought the land and began to excavate. We went around the site with a knowledgeable guide. He pointed out a place where there had been a small octagonal Byzantine church. Beneath that they found evidence of a smaller, simpler church of the first centuries of Christianity. And below that they had found the foundation of a house that was thought to be Simon Peter's.

In front of it ran a street with ancient stones. Along it other sites were being excavated. At the end of the street were the remains of a large Byzantine church, below which had been found a mosaic floor with ancient Jewish symbols. Our guide dated it back to the time of Jesus. We were not allowed to stand on the floor, but I could visualize the events that had taken place. I could hear Jesus speaking to the crowd and later rebuking the demon in the unfortunate man who had shouted at him. Then I could see Jesus walking with his new disciples down the street we had just walked up, to Peter's house. I could see him entering the house that had stood on that small foundation, where Peter's mother-in-law lay ill.

The story of the calling of Simon and Andrew, James and John, in the first chapter of Mark has always seemed to me too stark to be the way it really happened. I am indebted to Larry Naber of Minneapolis for suggesting that the postresurrection story at the end of John (chapter 21) may well be closer to how it actually happened. I have let Zebedee tell it Mark's way, and given John's beautiful story to Simon.

As I reread the Gospels I am struck by how many times Jesus and his friends are by the sea or out in boats. Jesus sometimes preached from a boat to multitudes on the shore. At times he crossed the Sea of Galilee to the other side to get away from crowds. And Mark 4:35–41 tells how one time a great windstorm arose. Jesus was so at home on the sea that he continued to sleep in the stern of the boat. His friends woke him, saying, "Teacher, don't you care that we are perishing?" But he felt no fear, and it seemed to his friends that the sea responded to him, and they themselves lost their anxiety in the presence of his confidence.

Were other disciples beside Peter married? We do not know. As long as Jesus lived in Galilee, Simon Peter would not have been far from home and was probably there often enough to support his family and be part of their life. Of course everything changed once Jesus "set his face to go to Jerusalem."

Reflections

1. People in Capernaum said that Jesus spoke "with authority." Have you heard someone who spoke "with authority"? How did you recognize it?

2. Jesus' preaching attracted favorable attention in Capernaum, but not in Nazareth. What reason might there be for this?

3. What do you think was really wrong with the demoniac who shouted at Jesus in the synagogue?

4. The Gospels do not mention Peter's wife. How do you think he happened to be living with his mother-in-law? If he had a wife, why is she not mentioned? Do you think other disciples were married? Did they renounce their families when they agreed to follow Jesus? (See Matt. 10:37.)

5. Have you had experience living with a mother- or father-in-law, or a son- or daughter-in-law? Was it a positive experience,

or a frustrating one? Did it make for trouble between you
and your spouse?

6. If you had just been healed by Jesus, would you have gotten
up to feed everyone in sight, or would you have rested quietly and talked to Jesus?

7. How do you visualize Jesus calling the four young fishermen?

8. Have you had a sense of calling in your life?

CHAPTER 5

The Woman with a Hemorrhage

Mark 5:25–34; Luke 8:43–48; Matthew 9:20–22

As he went, the crowds pressed in on him. Now there was a woman who had been suffering from hemorrhages for twelve years; and though she had spent all she had on physicians, no one could cure her. She came up behind him and touched the fringe of his clothes, and immediately her hemorrhage stopped.

—LUKE 8:42b–44

If a woman conceives and bears a male child, she shall be ceremonially unclean seven days. . . . Her time of blood purification shall be thirty-three days. . . . If she bears a female child, she shall be unclean two weeks. . . . Her time of blood purification shall be sixty-six days.

When the days of her purification are completed, whether for a son or for a daughter, she shall bring to the priest at the entrance of the tent of meeting a lamb in its first year for a burnt offering, and a pigeon or a turtledove for a sin offering. He shall offer it before God, and make atonement on her behalf.

—LEVITICUS 12:2, 4a, 5–7a

The Story of the Woman with a Hemorrhage

I have never understood why girls cannot go to the synagogue, like boys, and learn to read the Torah. I always learned things as quickly as my brothers, sometimes more quickly. I went on the Sabbath to the synagogue with my mother. We stood in the women's section, away from the men. I heard the scripture read, first in Hebrew, then in our language. Over the years I learned many passages by heart.

Sometimes I did not understand a passage and would ask my father or one of my brothers what it meant, but they never would tell me. Girls are not supposed to understand, they said. One Sabbath I heard the opening passages of the first book of Moses, and I remember that the scribe read:

> Then God said, "Let us make humankind in our image, according to our likeness; . . ." So God created humankind in his image, in the image of God he created them; male and female he created them. God blessed them, and God said to them, "Be fruitful and multiply." (Gen. 1:26–28a)

I asked my father, if women as well as men are made in God's image, why is God so hard on women? Why is giving birth to a new human being unclean? Why are women unclean for thirty-three days after the birth of a son, and why is it twice that long after the birth of a daughter? And after that, a woman must bring a lamb or a pigeon or turtledove to the priest for a "sin offering," and the priest sacrifices the animal to God to make atonement for her. Atonement for what? In what way do women sin in giving birth? My father replied that our God is a God of justice, and I asked why the justice seemed to be only for the men. He said it was blasphemy for me to ask such questions. So I stopped asking, but I did not stop thinking.

If you think I sound bitter, hear my story.

When I was twelve, my father arranged a marriage to a good man for me. A year later I gave birth to our son. I was glad he was a boy, because I knew my husband was counting on a son. The birth was reasonably quick for a first birth, and our baby was perfect in every way. The midwife had difficulty stopping the flow of blood afterwards, but in time it ceased.

My energy returned and I felt at peace nursing and caring for our baby.

Shortly before the period of ritual uncleanness was to end, I climbed on a stool to reach a top shelf to get a blanket to cover the baby. I lost my balance and fell, crashing into the corner of a cabinet. I was stunned by the fall and had a hard time getting back to my feet. I could feel that ribs were broken. Every movement was painful, but I knew the ribs would heal in time. And then I became aware of the bleeding. I was unclean again. I sat there and cried.

When my husband came home, he went for the midwife. She came with her herbs and made potions for me which I drank faithfully, but the bleeding did not stop. Months dragged on. Sometimes the flow lessened, and once it even stopped for a few days, but then it began again. I was drained of energy. It seemed the more I worried, the heavier the flow. But how do you stop worrying? I would tell myself to concentrate on how lucky I was to have an understanding husband and a beautiful baby, but the nagging questions came unbidden. What if the blood never stops? What if my husband leaves me? What will happen to my baby? How can I keep from making him unclean?

But I was young. At times the force of life was so strong in me I felt that surely I would wake some morning and find myself clean again. Or I would find a physician who could heal me. Some miracle would happen. This was not the end of my life.

Everything was difficult, however. It was hard to keep clean. I could no longer bathe in the river, or wash my clothes there. If I went out of the house, people avoided me, afraid I might brush against them and make them unclean. Even close friends shunned me.

I realized I had to protect my child. I asked a cousin who was nursing a baby of her own to take my precious little son. He has grown up in her family. I have seen him only once in a while from a distance because I don't want to make him unclean. Twelve long years have passed.

My son went to Jerusalem for the Passover this year, but I could not go to rejoice with him. Even if I could have avoided touching him, I would not have the strength for such a journey. He is a man now, and I have missed all these years of his life.

My husband was patient and sympathetic, but in time he divorced me. I do not blame him. We could no longer share the same bed. We no longer had a normal life together. He made a generous settlement of money, more than enough to meet my needs. He soon married again and now has several children. He has continued to take an interest in me and to help out when he can.

I have also been blessed with two good neighbors. My husband has given one of them money to shop for food at the market for me. The other has brought water from the well every day. I have not touched them, but we have talked together so I have not felt utterly alone. They are always suggesting new remedies for me to try and bringing me news of healers or physicians coming into the area.

When I heard of a physician in a neighboring town, I would walk there slowly. I would pull my mantle over my face so people would not recognize me. The physicians were all men, of course, and would not come near me once they heard the nature of my illness. Sometimes they had suggestions. I tried their potions. I bought their ointments. One of them suggested exercises, but I was too weak to do much. Nothing helped. None of them had any real feeling for what I was going through. I "endured much under many physicians, and . . . spent all that I had, and . . . was no better, but rather grew worse" (Mark 5:26).

My husband consulted some of the rabbis on my behalf, since they too were afraid I might contaminate them. They all said I must search my conscience. I must have committed some grievous sin to be so severely punished. If I would just confess, they would know the proper sacrifice so I could buy God's forgiveness and be healed. I lay awake nights, going over every detail of my life, even minor things, and I could find nothing deserving such long-lasting and terrible punishment. They suggested prayers for me to recite. They would make sacrifices for me, even without knowing the nature of my sin. I bought doves, and once a lamb, but this did not heal me any more than the physicians' remedies. I know how Job felt. And like Job, I had "comforters" who were of no comfort.

Then my neighbors came in one day in great excitement to say that a rabbi with the gift of healing was coming to our town. His name is Jesus, they said, and he has healed many lepers and people possessed by demons. He cares about outcasts and people who suffer. Large crowds follow him, for he not only heals but preaches and interprets scripture.

Hope soared in me. I wondered how I could approach him without contaminating him. I lay awake and thought about it from every angle I could imagine. Perhaps I could mingle with the crowd and get close to him. Perhaps merely touching his garment would be sufficient, since his power is so great.

Jesus came the next day. I dressed carefully in clothes I had not worn since my bleeding began. I pulled my mantle over my face and joined the crowd at the center of our town. Slowly I worked my way closer until I was right behind him. I knelt down and touched the fringe of his robe. Immediately I felt a great shock go through me. I felt the bleeding stop. The miracle had happened. Now if I could just get back home without being recognized.

Before I could move, I heard Jesus say, "Who touched me?" One of the men with him said, "Rabbi, just look at the crowd around you. How can you ask who touched you?" He responded, "I felt the power go out of me. Someone touched me and was healed." I had indeed felt that power enter my own body. I knew I had to tell him what I had done. He would probably denounce me for making him unclean.

With fear and trembling I knelt before him. I briefly told him my story, still expecting to be rebuked. His voice was gentle beyond belief. "Daughter of Sarah, your faith has made you whole. Go in peace."

I looked up into his face and rather boldly said, "If faith alone were enough, Rabbi, I would have been healed long ago. I needed your gift of healing, your grace and understanding, along with my faith, to make me whole again."

He reached down and took me by the hand and helped me to my feet. Several men nearby gasped. They still thought I was unclean and backed away from me. Jesus told them I had suffered long enough. I marveled. Who was this man who felt he could set aside the law of Moses? Friends, neighbors, even strangers came up to me, rejoicing with me. They were not worried that I was still unclean. What Jesus had said and done was enough for them. They welcomed me back into the community.

I knew I would have to burn all my bedding and clothing and scrub the whole house—walls, floors, and every piece of furniture. But the neighbors came by to rejoice with me without waiting for the big cleaning. My husband heard the news and came bringing our son. I was afraid the boy would feel strange with me, but he embraced me without hesitation. He will be married soon. My husband gave me money to buy new clothes and something special to wear to the wedding. Other people brought food, and there was a wonderful celebration.

Jesus spent several days in our town, speaking to people in the evening near the well. I went each evening, wanting to learn everything I could. He told us God is not far off, not judgmental. God is near at hand, like a father who wants fullness of life for everyone, for we are all his children. Jesus said that rules were made to help people live together in peace. If they are no longer helpful, they should be set aside. Someone asked what the most important rule to try to keep is, and he answered:

"You shall love . . . your God with all your heart, and with all your soul, and with all your mind." This is the greatest and first commandment. And a second is like it: "You shall love

your neighbor as yourself." On these two commandments hang
all the law and the prophets. (Matt. 22:37–40)

Everyone stood silent, thinking about all he had said. I felt
that I had been waiting all my life for just this message. I was
full of hope for the years that lay ahead and the new life I
would be able to enjoy. Then, before we parted for the night,
he read from the scroll of the prophet Isaiah where God says
to his people: "As a mother comforts her child, so I will comfort you; you shall be comforted" (Isa. 66:13).

It seems to me now that God comes to us according to our
need. Sometimes God is like a father, strong and steadfast,
standing between us and disaster. And sometimes God is like
the comfort of a mother's lap when everything has gone wrong.
But for me, now, God must be like Jesus!

Comments

For many years I found the healing miracles something of a
problem. I simply did not believe them.

Then I met John Calvi, who is trained and licensed in mas-
sage and has the gift of healing in his hands. He is a member
of the Friends Meeting in Putney, Vermont. He has found that
though he cannot cure AIDS, he can relieve the pain. His
Friends Meeting, believing in the genuineness and importance
of his gift, undertakes to support him—an effort in which many
of us join—so that he may spend full time working with AIDS
patients and with victims of torture, for whom he also has a
special concern. In addition, he teaches others how to help
relieve pain.

Knowing John, and having experienced myself the healing
power in his hands, I have come to understand more clearly
how Jesus healed. It is by a transfer of power and energy from
the healer to the person being healed. It requires in the healer
the willingness to be involved in another's suffering, and also

the willingness to be drained or used up. "The power has gone out of me," said Jesus. It is exhausting work, and from time to time the healer is in need of healing. It requires in the person being healed faith that the healing can take place, active participation, and a sense of selfhood and self-worth: the conviction that one's life is important and worthy of being brought back to wholeness.

Because in other stories we find Jesus from time to time setting aside the law, I felt he would ignore the rules regarding impurity in order to restore this woman immediately to her community.

The Christian Church continued many of the taboos against women that were prevalent in the time of Jesus. Yet, when we turn to the Gospels, we find Jesus breaking many of them and setting women free of the limitations their religion placed on them. We find him making them equal partners in his new movement.

One of my reasons for writing these stories has been to show how Jesus, as we see him in the Gospels, cut through the petty restrictions that women had to live with and broke taboo after taboo against them in his own day. This story is a good example.

Reflections

1. What reason could there be to consider a woman unclean after giving birth to a child? Why was she considered unclean twice as long after the birth of a girl as after the birth of a boy? Who established these rules, and for what purpose?

2. What taboos against women exist today?

3. Jesus broke many taboos against women in his own day. What reason could there be for the church that grew up in his name to deny women full status within it? What would prompt a celibate clergy to establish rules about women's personal lives?

4. This woman was shunned by her community for a dozen years. Have you ever felt ostracized by people, or have you known someone who has been? How long did the situation last? Was it resolved? If so, how?

5. Have you ever felt someone draining you of energy and power? What did you do? Were you able to grow beyond this in the relationship with that person?

6. Have you ever felt empowered by someone to do or be more than you thought yourself capable of? Was it a lasting empowerment? Have you been able to empower someone? How?

7. Jesus set aside the law of Moses regarding the ritual cleansing period after an uncleanness and restored the woman to her community immediately. Was he right to do this? By what authority did he break the law?

8. Have you ever broken a law for conscience' sake? What happened?

CHAPTER 6

The Syrophoenician Woman

Mark 7:24–30 (see also Matthew 15:21–28)

❧

And from there [Jesus] arose and went away to the region of
Tyre and Sidon. And he entered a house, and would not have
anyone know of it, yet he could not be hid. But immediately
a woman, whose little daughter was possessed by an unclean
spirit, heard of him, and came and fell down at his feet. Now
the woman was a Greek, a Syrophoenician by birth. And she
begged him to cast the demon out of her daughter.

—MARK 7:24–26 RSV[1]

The Syrophoenician Woman's Story

I have lived all my life in Tyre, the great seaport of Syria built
by the Phoenicians. It was originally an island off the Syrian
coast in the Great Sea, a very ancient and prosperous community whose ships sailed as far west as Spain.

About three hundred years ago, Alexander the Great conquered Tyre, destroying much of the city in the process. He
built a causeway to the island so his troops could have a direct
connection. Sand has accumulated around the causeway,
making it now more than half a mile wide. We're really part of
the mainland now. After Tyre was subdued, Alexander rebuilt
it as a Greek city, as he did with other cities in other parts of
the world. Some of my ancestors came here at that time. We
Greeks still constitute a large community. We have our own

temples, and among ourselves we speak Greek, although in this cosmopolitan city we all speak several languages. There are many different national groups.

A century ago Tyre became part of the Roman Empire, which turned out to be advantageous to Tyrians as well as Romans. Tyre was able to retain some autonomy, and the city has prospered. We Greeks have kept our position among the cultural leaders of the city.

My early life wasn't very happy. My father was a sailor and went down with his ship when I was quite young. My mother, who had never been strong, grieved her life away and soon died also. My brother, Peter, and I went to live with an uncle and became part of his large, chaotic family. We never went hungry, but I always wore hand-me-down clothes and never had anything pretty of my own. When I was older, I asked my aunt to teach me to sew, and I picked up embroidery by watching her and experimenting. Now I could make clothes for myself.

Tyre is the great shipbuilding center at this end of the Great Sea. Other building trades are also highly developed here. Tyrian woodworkers and stonemasons are in demand far beyond the borders of our country. My brother was apprenticed to a carpenter and has done quite well. He has worked in many parts of the empire, as well as at home.

I am not bad-looking, and my uncle found a good husband for me, an honest and kindly man who treated me well. He was also strong and hardworking. He worked in the shipyards, where his tasks were difficult and dangerous. For all his strength he was always tender with me, even though he teased me. We laughed a lot and I learned to tease back. We were very happy.

Before long we were expecting our first child. He was excited about the son he felt sure we would have. Then shortly before the baby was born, he was crushed by a falling timber and died in a few days. It seemed like the end of the world to me.

In my loneliness and grief I gave birth to a little girl. I had wanted a daughter but just assumed it would be a boy, since my husband's heart was set on a son. When the midwife had cleaned up the baby, she laid her in my lap. I had expected her to be red, even ugly, as I had known new babies to be. I was surprised and amazed to find that she was beautiful. Then she opened her eyes and I saw that they were deep violet in color. I held her close and felt her respond. I named her Zoe, which means "life," for I felt that she had given me back my life.

After a period of working on the new summer palace for Herod in Tiberias in Galilee, Peter had some time off and was free to help me find a little house in the small Greek community on the outskirts of town. It is on the main road into the city and not expensive. It has been a good place for Zoe and me. Before he was married, Peter lived with us when he was home.

I knew women who supported themselves, working at home, making clothes for people. I felt sure I could do that, too, since I have a talent for sewing and embroidery. When Zoe grew out of swaddling clothes, I made her little tunics and embroidered them with flowers, often in purple, the Tyrian color, and Zoe's color too. When we went to the well or the market, women noticed my beautiful daughter and her lovely clothes, and soon I had as much business as I could handle.

We have good neighbors next door. The woman is about my age. Her name is Eunice, which means "fair victory." She has a girl about Zoe's age named Irene, which means "peace," and a boy three years older named George, which means "farmer," or "lover of the earth." The children play together happily and George takes good care of the girls. He seems to love them both. The father is a merchant and gone from home for long stretches of time. Eunice and I are good friends and look after each other's children so that we both have more time to ourselves.

Right from the beginning I seemed to understand Zoe from the inside. I knew how she felt and what it took to make her happy. I could explain things to her so that she understood and would cooperate. Discipline was never a problem. She has wisdom beyond her years. She became my friend and teacher. She knew how to comfort me when I was discouraged. She grew more beautiful with each passing year, and was maturing rapidly. I realized I ought to begin to think about arranging a marriage for her. I dreaded the time when she would leave our little house and I would be alone again.

And then she began to fade before my eyes. She had always loved to help me, but now even simple tasks were beyond her. She who had had such grace, such joy in life, now found it hard to get out of bed.

In alarm I sent for a physician. He said that a powerful demon had possession of her. He was familiar with demons that cause seizures and demons that cause paralysis, but this demon he did not know. He suggested a potion. Eunice bought the herbs and helped me make it. We tried it faithfully, but Zoe grew no better.

She lay on her pallet day after day. Her skin grew pale, then chalk white. Her eyes lost their luster. Then the bleeding began, first from her nose, and later from her gums. I was now afraid she would die. I tried every doctor in the city. One knew about a physician in Sidon, the other major Phoenician city. I sent a messenger with money, and the doctor came. But he had never seen this demon before either. Again we tried the pills and potions he suggested, but I could see that even he did not think they would cure her.

I went to the temple and made offerings. I prayed to Demeter, who had grieved for her daughter Persephone, carried off to the underworld. I also prayed and made sacrifices to Aesclepius, the god of healing. I talked to the attendant at the temple. She told me that Aesclepius had said, "Only the wounded can heal." I thought back on the physicians we had consulted and wondered if any of them had ever really been wounded. They seemed to have so little feeling for what we were facing. They were too eager to get out of the house and go on to less difficult cases.

Zoe grew weaker and at times was unconscious. I watched by her bed at night, bathing her with cool water. My neighbor often watched in the day while I tried to rest, but I was too worried to sleep much. Our money was dwindling, but I could not concentrate on work. My fear of losing Zoe blotted out everything else.

One day Eunice rushed in, quite excited. She had heard that a man from Galilee, known far and wide for his healing power, had left his own country and was in ours. It was thought he would be coming to Tyre. I vaguely remembered that my brother had mentioned such a man when he returned from working in Galilee. I thought he said his name is Joshua, or Jesus in Greek.

I usually prefer not to be around Jewish people, for they think they are the chosen race. Of course, I know that we Greeks feel superior too. However, if this man were really a powerful healer, I would be humble before him. I had heard that they use the phrase "Son of David" for their expected Messiah. I would call him that if I were able to talk to him.

Now Eunice heard that he was coming into Tyre on our very road. Even as she spoke, we heard the noise of a crowd in the distance. She urged me to go. I pulled on my mantle and rushed out. I could see the crowd now, stopped in front of a house which I remembered belonged to a Jewish family.

In the midst of the crowd, I saw a tall man who seemed to be the center of attention. He was about to enter the house. I rushed up, elbowing my way through the crowd, and cried out, "Son of David, have mercy on me. My daughter is possessed by a demon." He did not answer me. I pushed my way a little nearer and was able to fall at his feet. I tugged at his robe to get his attention. "Son of David," I cried again, "my daughter will die if you do not help me." People shouted me down. They urged him to send me away and began shoving me. I was being a nuisance.

I stopped pleading and looked at this man, and I was shocked by what I saw. He was utterly exhausted. His face had little color and he seemed near collapse. Had he come to our beautiful seaside city in need of rest and healing himself? Had he hoped no one would recognize him in another country? My pity went out to him. For a moment I considered whether I should just go home and leave him alone. But when I thought of Zoe, I knew I could not give up.

Then I remembered Aesclepius. Was this the wounded healer?

Once again I tugged at his garment. "Sir," I said quietly, "she is all that I have." I saw that he did not have the strength to do what I asked. He seemed a bit confused.

Now he looked over my head, not seeing me, and said coldly, "I did not come to heal your people. I was sent only to the lost sheep of the house of Israel." I clung to him, imploring him to help, but he simply did not see me. I was the stranger, the outsider, the nuisance. Again he looked over my head and said, "It is not right to give the children's bread to dogs." The word calls up hordes of wild dogs, roaming the streets, feeding on garbage, and licking the sores of the beggars and lepers. He hesitated over the word, and gave it the diminutive ending, making it little dogs, or puppies. I saw hope in this.

If he expected me to slink away, he would be disappointed. I stood up now and looked directly at him. I said quietly, "Sir, even the little dogs under the table are nourished by the crumbs that fall from the children."

Now he looked at me and our eyes met. I saw surprise, perhaps even admiration, on his face. I watched him as he gathered his energy. The exhaustion seemed to fall from him. He looked at me now with kindness and said quietly, "For what you have just said, go your way in peace. Your daughter is healed."

Somehow I believed him. I bowed in thanks, pushed my way through the crowd, and ran back home. It was true! Zoe was still lying on her bed, but the color had returned to her face and the brightness to her eyes. "Mother," she said, "I'm hungry."

While she ate I told her everything that had happened. She said she must see him herself and thank him for giving her back her life. I suggested we wait until morning, but she was afraid he might leave early. How could I refuse her anything on this day?

She washed herself and took a little time to choose a clean tunic to wear, a purple one. She looked lovely and like herself again. We walked together in the twilight to the house where I had encountered him. I hoped he had had time to rest.

I knocked and asked the man who opened the door if we might speak to Jesus for a moment. He hesitated, but Jesus heard us and came to the door himself. Zoe thanked him a bit shyly, but with her usual grace. I told him that our Greek god of healing, Aesclepius, had said, "Only the wounded can heal." He listened thoughtfully and nodded his head. He said that the Hebrew prophet Isaiah had foretold that the Messiah would be a *suffering servant*, "a man of sorrows, and acquainted with grief" (Isa. 53:3b KJV).[2] Isaiah had also said that the Messiah would be a healer:

> Then the eyes of the blind shall be opened,
> and the ears of the deaf unstopped;
> Then the lame shall leap like a deer,
> and the tongue of the speechless sing for joy.
>
> —ISAIAH 35:5–6

He blessed Zoe, and I knelt so that he could bless me too. He thanked us for coming, and we took our leave.

On the way home, Zoe said to me, "Mother, I must get on with my life. It is time to get married. I want to marry George, the boy next door, not some stranger. We have always loved each other." And I thought, why not? Later we talked it over with our neighbors. Everyone was excited and happy with the idea.

We are all planning a wedding for spring. George and Zoe and Irene spend time roaming the neighborhood, looking for a little house. Zoe and Irene are excited that they will be sisters now. And I won't lose Zoe after all. I look forward to being a mother-in-law, and a grandmother!

Sometimes at night I lie awake in wonder and gratitude. I think how the wounded healer finally came to us, not one of our own people, but a member of a group I had avoided. I think with humility that I helped him see that his message and his gift of healing are for everyone, not just his own people. And I am glad that I am Greek, with a long, rich heritage and enough self-confidence to speak for myself, and enough pride not to be humiliated by an insult.

When your child's life hangs in the balance, you find resources in yourself that you didn't know you had. You can demand help from a stranger too exhausted to treat you with courtesy. When we parted, Jesus said, "Ask, and it will be given you; search, and you will find; knock, and the door will be opened for you" (Matt. 7:7).

Comments

When I read this story in the New Revised Standard Version, I was astonished to find the woman called "a Gentile of Syrophoenician origin." The word in the Greek Testament is *Hellenis,* which seems clearly to mean "Greek." I rushed to my Strong's Exhaustive Concordance, which says, "Hellenis, fem. A Grecian (i.e., non-Jewish) woman: Greek."

I checked other translations. The Jerusalem Bible and Moffatt both use "pagan." The Good News Bible says "foreigner." Lamsa's Aramaic translation calls her "heathen."

I have a personal investment in this story. As far as I am concerned the woman is Greek, a Hellenic woman, as the Greek Testament states. For this reason I am using Mark's version of the story rather than Matthew's, since Matthew calls her a "Canaanite." Luke does not tell this story, perhaps because it portrays Jesus in a rather unfavorable light. He insults a woman, and then lets her have the last word!

When Jesus responds to the woman and heals her daughter, Matthew has him use the stock phrase "Great is your faith." In Mark, Jesus says, "For saying that, you may go—the demon 'has left your daughter" (Mark 7:29). That, I think, has the ring of truth.

In the story that precedes this one, about the woman with a hemorrhage, healing takes place when she touches the hem of his garment. In this one the girl is not present. The psychological link may be enough for healing. At times when I have been seriously ill, I have felt the energy of individuals and groups who were praying for me, or, as Quakers say, "holding me in the Light."

For years I wondered how Jesus could be so unfeeling as to call another human being a dog, even a little dog. Then I saw how this story is linked to the preceding one. When the woman with a hemorrhage touched his garment, Jesus was aware of it and said, "The power has gone out of me."

The Gospels report many healings. If the power went out of him with each one, he must from time to time have been so depleted that he was in need of rest and healing himself. I remember times when I have been utterly exhausted and failed to treat people with courtesy. I came to understand how even Jesus could be discourteous. He leaves his own country, hoping for a time of rest and solitude. No one here will know him, he thinks. Herod's men were always hoping to find some excuse to arrest him. In Syrophoenicia he is out of their jurisdiction. "He entered a house and did not want anyone to know he was there" (Mark 7:24b). The pushy Greek woman seemed like the last straw.

The greatness of Jesus shines through this story. He does not argue with the woman. He is willing for her to have the last word. He is truly humble. (I like the definition of humility from the twelve-step programs: "Humility is the willingness to become teachable.") Jesus is willing to learn from a woman, even a gentile, a Greek woman.

Reflections

1. Why do you think some translators of the Gospels used such words as "foreigner," "pagan," and "heathen" for the Syro-

phoenician woman, when the Greek seems quite clear in calling her merely "a Greek woman"?

2. Some groups today still send missionaries to convert people from their own native religions to Christianity. Is it possible to have dialogue and mutual sharing of belief and practices without separating people from their own spiritual traditions?

3. Does it lessen Jesus in your opinion that he insulted the woman in the story by calling her a "dog"?

4. Do you think the woman was justified in talking back to Jesus? What gave her the strength to do it? Should Jesus have let her have the last word?

5. What would you have done or said if you had been in her place? Have you ever been insulted by someone? How did you feel? Do you still carry scars from the experience?

6. With Peter's mother-in-law, Jesus had physical contact in healing her. With the woman with a hemorrhage, touching his clothing was sufficient. In this story, the girl is healed, though she is not physically present. How did Jesus heal? What is the common element in these stories?

7. Have you ever been part of a spiritual healing group? Have you experienced "spiritual healing"?

CHAPTER 7

The Mother of the Sons of Zebedee

Matthew 20:20–28, 27:55–56

He set his face to go to Jerusalem.

—Luke 9:51b

Then the mother of the sons of Zebedee came to him with her sons, and kneeling before him, she asked a favor of him.

—Matthew 20:20

The Story of the Mother of the Sons of Zebedee

I've been just another housewife, going along, doing my work, gossiping with other women at the well. I've complained about things I didn't understand, more loudly than most, but I really don't have much to complain about. Zebedee's a good man, as good as any in Capernaum. He's been a wonderful father to our children, and he has built his fishing into a prosperous business. We've never wanted for anything.

I was married when I was twelve, and before the year was out we had a child. Zebedee was disappointed that it was a girl, but he didn't say much. Two more daughters followed in succession. Zebedee began to worry. Men always want sons.

Five long years went by and no more children. Our girls have been a great joy, but they could not make up to Zebedee for a son. Then at last God answered our prayers and gave us a son. Zebedee was overjoyed and named him James. And do you know what that name means? It means "usurper"! James would now usurp his sisters' place in Zebedee's affection. The girls laughed about it and took it as a joke. The next year our second son was born. Zebedee gave him a name I liked better, John, which means "God is gracious." It has been a good name for that son, for he has always been a lovable and loving person, a joy to have around.

Zebedee boasted of his sons all over town. When I went to the well for water, the other women teased me and called me "the mother of the sons of Zebedee"! I always said, "No, I'm the mother of Zebedee's children, both daughters and sons." Their father loved the boys so much he found it hard to discipline them, so they grew up boisterous and uninhibited. Later Jesus called them "sons of thunder" because they were so noisy. There was always laughter and fun where they were, and everyone loved them.

Our house is on the main street of Capernaum, the one with the synagogue at the end. We've had good neighbors next door, a man named Simon and his family. He's also in the fishing business, with his brother Andrew, who also spends a great deal of time at Simon's house.

Simon's wife, a girl from our town, seemed to run out of energy after her children began to come. Her mother moved in with them and does most of the work. Frankly, she's too old to work that hard. I've wondered whether there is anything wrong with Simon's wife except laziness. I'd never say that to her mother, because she and I are very good friends. I enjoy her company. She's much quieter than I am and is something of a worrier. What she says, however, often has some depth to it and gives me something to think about.

My life is much easier now that our children are grown. Our girls all have families of their own. Zebedee and I just love being grandparents. The boys are still young, and we've not pushed them into marriage. Zebedee really likes to have them around. They help with the fishing and he hopes they will take over the business when he can't work any more.

My neighbor worries about her son-in-law being a radical, and she has had good reason to be concerned. Simon and his brother actually went down to Judea to investigate a new prophet preaching at the ford in the Jordan River. They wanted our boys to go with them, but their father talked some sense into them and they stayed home. And a good thing, too! Simon and Andrew were gone for weeks. The prophet was arrested and later put to death. Simon and his brother came back to Capernaum somewhat discouraged. I know that Simon's mother-in-law hoped he would settle down now.

One day the gossip at the well was all about a new rabbi who had moved into a little house on the edge of town. People said he'd been run out of his hometown. My neighbor and I sensed trouble, and it came all too soon.

The next morning Zebedee came home from fishing without the boys. He was upset. He reported that they'd gone off with this new rabbi and just left their father sitting in the boat. Our neighbor came over. She said that Simon and Andrew had not come home either. When she heard what Zebedee said, she looked so stricken I put my arm around her to comfort her. She was burning up with fever. I helped her back home and put her to bed. Her daughter finally got up to take over so her mother could rest.

The new rabbi preached in our synagogue the next morning. His name is Joshua, or Jesus, as many people call him. The whole town turned out to hear him. I was crowded in with the other women at the back and had trouble hearing him. I left early, wanting to look in on my sick neighbor. I found her no better, perhaps a little worse. I did what I could to make her comfortable.

After a time we heard people coming down the street. I went to the door and heard Simon pointing out his house to the rabbi. I thought to myself, that's all his mother-in-law needs, to have a stranger and half the town gathering when she's so sick. Zebedee turned in at our house and motioned to me to come home. He was obviously shaken. He said that this Jesus taught with authority. He scolded me for leaving so soon. He said Jesus made his points by telling stories that made people laugh, but they got the message even so.

I went to the door and found the crowd outside Simon's house growing. People were buzzing with the news that Jesus had healed Simon's mother-in-law quite miraculously. They said that she was out of bed and serving food, not only to her family, but to everyone in sight. Just like her! I've never known anyone with such a strong sense of duty.

People were bringing their sick and crippled, and Jesus stood in the doorway and healed them. Even I was impressed by what I saw. Finally the crowd dispersed. I hoped our boys would have sense enough to come home now, but no, they went right along with their new teacher and spent the night at his house.

The next day I asked Zebedee what he intended to do about his sons. He said crossly that he did not intend to do anything about them. They were grown now and could make their own decisions. If they chose to follow Jesus, he would not stand in their way. After all, he said, Jesus might be the Messiah. He did not want to talk to me about it. He stalked out of the house, and I knew it was no use trying to talk sense into him then.

I went next door. My friend seemed quite recovered and less anxious than usual. She told me how she had felt strength go through her when Jesus raised her to her feet. Her energy had come back. She called it a miracle. I asked her how she felt about Simon and Andrew going off like that. She said she was glad they are followers of Jesus. I commented that it would be hard to get along with the men gone, and she merely said, "We'll manage." There was no use talking to her either.

Jesus kept calling more people to be his followers. Now the gossip at the well was that some of them are women. I was shocked. What kind of messiah would call women? And what kind of women would travel around the countryside with a bunch of fishermen? Word of more miraculous healings reached our town, and people repeated some of the parables that Jesus told. I had to admit they were good stories.

Once when Jesus and his followers came back to Capernaum, so many wanted to hear him preach that the synagogue could not hold them all. He asked people to gather on the shore. Then he climbed into Simon's boat and rowed out a bit. His voice carried over the water and people listened intently. I was there too. I didn't hear him say anything about a revolution!

Afterward at the well I met some of the women who travel with him. They were not at all what I expected. They were all modestly dressed and seemed respectable. One of them came up and talked to me. Her name is Mary and she comes from Magdala, another fishing village not far from here. She introduced me to others. Some of them are as old as I am. I liked them. But still I wondered why Jesus needed women in his group. They wouldn't be much help in fighting the Roman legions!

One day James and John came home and said that the whole group would go to Jerusalem in the spring and celebrate the Passover there. They were already planning the journey, months ahead. They expected that there would probably be some confrontation with the authorities. I learned that Jesus had called more than seventy people. This sounded as though he meant business at last. I said I would like to meet him before they left. The boys suggested that we go right away. I walked with them to the little house where Jesus has his headquarters.

He was in the courtyard. I picked a moment when he seemed unoccupied. I went up very respectfully and knelt before him, motioning to my sons to kneel with me. "Sir," I said, "my husband and I have given our sons to your movement. We have not had their help and support for weeks at a time. This has gone on now for almost three years. Now I want to ask something of you." He asked what I wanted, and with pride in my voice I said, "Promise me that when you come into power, my sons will sit, one at your right hand and one at your left."

He looked at me sadly and said, "You don't know what you are asking." The others gathered around, complaining about James and John wanting special places. Jesus held up his hands for silence. "You know," he said, "that the rulers of the Gentiles lord it over them, and their great ones are tyrants over them. It will not be so among you, but whoever wishes to be great among you must be your servant."

Then he looked at me and said that God's reign is not like Caesar's. Rather, it is a *community*, where everyone is called by name. It is for the poor and the oppressed, outcasts and prisoners, the sick and those who mourn. And, he added, it is for women and children too. He was talking directly to me, but everyone was listening intently. And finally I understood. He looked around the group and said, "I have called you friends" (John 15:15). Then he added, "I am among you as one who serves" (Luke 22:27).

I knelt there on the hard ground and tears ran down my cheeks. I was blinded by this vision of a new world in which women are called by name and respected, where children live unafraid, where poor people have enough to eat, where lepers are healed and prisoners set free, where no one has power over the others, but we all have power together. He quoted the prophet Isaiah, who had written:

They will not hurt or destroy on all my holy mountain;
for the earth will be full of the knowledge of [God]
as the waters cover the sea.

—ISAIAH 11:9[1]

Everyone was quiet. He reached out his hand to me and drew me to my feet. Then he called me by name and asked, "Will you follow me too?" I nodded my head, not trusting myself to speak. He said to me, "You are no longer just the mother of the sons and daughters of Zebedee. You are God's daughter, a member of God's community." I blurted out, "Can I go to Jerusalem with you?" He smiled and said, "I want very much for you to come with us."

Back home I talked to my neighbor. She said, "You go! I will look after Zebedee. I'll cook his meals and see that he has clean clothes." When Zebedee came home and I told him all that had happened, he too said, "You go! You can keep an eye on our boys so they won't get into trouble." And I know that he told James and John to keep an eye on me too!

I spend nights at home now, but in the day I am with Jesus and the others as we make our plans. Jesus says we will be too conspicuous if we all travel together. We will go in pairs and be responsible for our partners. I'm going with Susanna. I have come to love her. We are spiritual friends and pray together each day. I really love all the women. They do not gossip like the women in Capernaum. They have dignity and a sense of purpose. I want to be like them.

Some of them are poor, and some, like Joanna and Susanna, must have come from wealth. They really provide for Jesus and his friends, and I will be able to help them. We all look to Mary Magdalene, who is close to Jesus. She's truly humble, and a friend to everyone.

We are all anxious about what may happen in Jerusalem. But I am determined to be a follower of Jesus to the end. I will not turn back. I will not desert him.

It is strange how life sometimes gives you something you wanted but seemed to lose. I had foolishly wanted special places for my sons in Jesus' movement when I thought he would start a revolution and come to power. Now it is apparent to me that our younger son John has a special place in his teacher's heart. I've heard people speak of him as "the disciple Jesus loves."

John continues to amaze me. From a loud, fun-loving boy, he has grown into a man of great depth. He is making notes about what Jesus says and does, so that someday, when he is old, he can write it all down in a book. Then people of all the generations to come will know about Jesus. Sometimes he says such beautiful things it takes my breath away. Just last night when he was talking to Zebedee and me about Jesus, he said, "In him is life, and the life is the light of all people. The light shines in the darkness and the darkness will never overcome it" (John 1:4–5).[2]

I don't want to be a loudmouthed, gossiping housewife any longer. From now on, I don't want to talk off the top of my head, the way I've done for so many years. I want my words to come out of the depths of truth within me. I want to be a child of the Light. I pray that I may learn to walk in the Light day after day, wherever it may lead me, even to the end of the world. I want to be worthy to live a new life in the community of God. Let it be.

Comments

A different version of this story appears in Mark 10:35–45. There James and John, by themselves, ask for the special places. It hardly seems possible that two of the original group of disciples, one of them "the disciple Jesus loves," could have misunderstood so badly the nature of the movement Jesus had started, particularly after traveling with him for three years. Matthew softens the story by having their mother ask. Matthew's Gospel is the only one to mention her.

Only a woman richly blessed with chutzpah could have asked for such an outrageous thing. I have tried to portray her as breezy and uninhibited. I'm confident, however, that in the end she did understand what the community Jesus wanted to establish was all about and entered the new movement wholeheartedly. Matthew includes her in the group of women present at the crucifixion. She did make the long trip to Jerusalem.

According to tradition, the Fourth Gospel was written by John the disciple. It is full of vivid details, like an eyewitness account. However, most scholars today do not think that Zebedee's son actually wrote it. They place the writing later.

For the sake of the story, however, I have let John plan to write the Fourth Gospel.

Likewise, "the disciple Jesus loved," mentioned five times in the Gospel of John, is by tradition this same John. I have included his closeness to Jesus in this story. But I think a case can be made that Mary Magdalene was really the "disciple Jesus loved." I will try to make that case in chapter 11.

Reflections

1. If, as the author suggests, Zebedee and his wife had daughters as well as sons, why is she not called "the mother of Zebedee's children"?

2. Do you treat boys differently from girls? Do societal and religious attitudes sometimes unconsciously dictate treating them differently?

3. Why do you think James and John would let their mother make such an outrageous request? In Mark's version, they ask it for themselves. How could they have misunderstood so completely the nature of Jesus' mission? Or is this a flaw in the writing of the story?

4. Why do you think Zebedee let his wife and sons go off with Jesus to Jerusalem? If he was convinced of the rightness of Jesus' mission, why didn't he go too?

5. In Matthew 20:25–28, Jesus gives a clear picture of the new order he hopes to establish. Does "kingdom of God" seem to fit what he is saying? Is your reaction colored by whether you live in a monarchy or a democracy?

6. If you had been writing these stories, would you have given names to all the women for whom the Gospels do not supply names? What name would you have given to the mother of the sons of Zebedee?

CHAPTER 8

The Bent-over Woman

Luke 13:10–22

❧

Jesus went through one town and village after another, teaching as he made his way to Jerusalem.

—LUKE 13:22

Now he was teaching in one of the synagogues on the sabbath. And just then there appeared a woman with a spirit that had crippled her for eighteen years. She was bent over and was quite unable to stand up straight.

—LUKE 13:10–11

The Bent-over Woman's Story

I remember my grandmother. She was my special friend when I was a little girl. Her back was bent over so that she could no longer stand up straight, and this put her down at my eye level. I could look right into her eyes and see her face light up with a smile. My mother was tall and straight, and I could see her face only when she bent down to me or picked me up and held me close.

Grandmother and I worked in the garden, growing food for the family. I loved to work with her because she sang while we worked. She taught me many of the beautiful songs that David the King gave us. In the spring we scratched the dirt and dug out the stones to make the ground ready for planting. Then we took the seeds we had carefully saved from the last harvest and buried them in the ground. After planting we watched each day, waiting for the first tiny green shoots to come up and pulling out the weeds before they could grow much. We planted beans and lentils, onions and leeks, cucumbers and melons. We also had grapevines. We ate much of the food we raised, and what we did not eat, we dried to use later. Then in the fall, the cycle began again. Two growing seasons a year meant that our work was never finished.

Tethered to a tree in the garden was a goat who gave us milk. She did not like to be petted, so I stayed away from her. Grandmother was always pointing out to me smaller creatures who shared the garden with us. We watched ants moving busily about, always in a hurry, but not getting in one another's way. If you stepped on an anthill, they set to work at once to repair the damage. There were also the earthworms. Grandmother said they ate their way through the soil, leaving it fine and workable for us. Once I cut one in two with my trowel and I felt sad when it died. Grandmother said that if I had hit a flatworm, both halves would have gone on as if nothing had happened. For her the garden was full of miracles. She knew all the birds by name, recognizing them by their songs since she could no longer look up to see them.

Sometimes I walked to the well or market with my mother and grandmother. People greeted us, and Grandmother called them by name. I wondered how she knew them, bent over as she was. She said she recognized people's feet. She knew the sandals they wore. Some were quite new, others worn; some were well cared for, even though worn. She knew the shape and condition of the bare feet, the well groomed and those with ragged nails. Some were quite clean, others mud encrusted. I began to watch feet as we walked. Soon I too could identify their owners.

Mother worked mostly in the house or, when the weather was nice, on the roof. Her life was very full. She made clothes for all of us. This included spinning the yarn, weaving the cloth, and sometimes dyeing it. Then she sewed it into tunics and robes for all of us. In the evening when it was still light, Grandmother often sewed with her. She embroidered pretty birds and flowers on my tunics and also helped with the mending. Mother prepared our food, going for water the first thing in the morning, making dough from barley kernels and setting it to rise, milking the goat and making curds and cheese. She pressed oil from olives to use in cooking and to fill our lamps. At times the demands of the garden meant that she worked with us there, but she did not sing, even when Grandmother and I sang.

I asked Grandmother why my mother did not sing. She told me that when mother was young, she was eager, full of hopes and dreams of how beautiful life could be. Then Grandmother's own back became more stooped, and finally she was so bent over that she could not do much but weed the garden. Mother had had to take over the main burden of endless housework. One by one her dreams were deferred, and then abandoned. She was married to someone not of her choice. Grandmother's own marriage had been happy, and she knew that this had made a great difference in her life. Then Mother began having babies. She wanted to be a good mother, but life was an endless round of work. Grandmother said to me, "Be kind to her. She needs all the help and love you can give her."

I began to take over some of the household work. I knew my mother loved me and wanted me to have a happy life, but she could not give me joy, for there was no joy left in her to give.

Year by year my mother became more stooped, and eventually she was bent over like Grandmother. Now the housework fell to me. I was determined not to lose my joy, so I sang while I cleaned and cooked and washed clothes.

Mother complained bitterly about the pain in her back. I was puzzled. Grandmother never talked about pain. I asked her if her back did not hurt, and she said that of course it did. She told me people differ in their capacity to bear pain and in their attitude toward it. She had found that if you accept pain, if you give in to it, it will keep its place as *part* of your life, but not all of existence. If you fight pain, it will always be stronger than you and won't let you think of anything else.[1]

Grandmother died, and we buried her in the family plot with other ancestors. The place seemed barren to me. I went back with mustard seeds, which grow quickly and become like a tree, but do not last. I also planted an olive pit, so that a real tree would grow.

Years passed. I grew up and was married too soon. When Mother died, we buried her beside Grandmother and the olive tree sheltered them both. It was quite big now. Birds came and built nests in it, and the whole area was lovely.

I gave birth to three daughters in a row. When I came to the end of the ritual period after the third birth, my husband angrily confronted me with my inability to bear sons. I tried to reason with him, but he stalked out of the house.

In anger and frustration I went out to the garden and began to weed furiously, muttering to myself. When I finished the plot on which I was working, I found I could not stand up. I cried out in fear and pain. My eldest daughter ran to me and rubbed my back with all her strength, wanting to help. I struggled and struggled to straighten my back, but it was no use. I was bent over too, only I was much younger than Mother and Grandmother were when the affliction overtook them.

I remembered what my grandmother had told me about pain. I tried to embrace it and to sing in spite of it. But my heart was full of bitterness, and my body no longer seemed under my control. I felt as if I were in alien country. How could I sing the songs of God in a strange land? (See Psalm 137:4.)

Eighteen years went by. Our daughters were married and grandsons came to bless our family. Finally, three years ago, a little granddaughter was born. She makes me think of myself at that age. She comes and peers into my face and smiles. In spite of the pain, I smile back at her. She helps me with the weeding.

One day my daughter came home from the well with news. A rabbi was traveling by easy stages from Galilee to Jerusalem and would be in our village on the Sabbath. The leader of our synagogue had sent word to him, inviting him to read and comment on the scripture. People said he could tell wonderful stories and explain the books of Moses and the prophets so that they seemed to come alive. They also said he had healed people whose condition seemed hopeless. My heart missed a beat. Was there hope for me? But no! He could not heal anyone on the Sabbath.

I had not gone much to the synagogue after my back became bent over, but I was eager to go this time. We arrived early, but already there was a crowd. I stood with my daughter and granddaughter in the women's section. I looked around at the feet and could call some of the women by name. Today the feet were all clean. This was a special Sabbath.

Soon the place became hushed, and I realized the rabbi must have come. I could imagine him sitting on the bench at the front of the men's section. I heard him ask for the scroll of the prophet Isaiah. He talked about how God had called Isaiah:

> to bring good news to the oppressed,
> to bind up the brokenhearted,
> to proclaim liberty to the captives,
> and release to the prisoners; . . .
> to comfort all who mourn . . .
>
> —ISAIAH 61:1b, 2b

He said that this was his calling also.

What a beautiful voice he had! I felt that he was speaking directly to me, but I knew that everyone else in the room must feel that also. I waited for his commentary, but it did not come.

He said, "Woman, come to me." The other women seemed to turn and look at me, but surely he could not mean me. How could I go to him in the men's section? Someone must have told him who I was, for he spoke again, calling me by name. People stood aside to make room for me and someone guided me, as I slowly made my way to the front of the men's section.

Now I was standing in front of him. I looked at his feet with tenderness.

He stood up and handed the scroll back to the leader of the synagogue. He put his hand on my back and slowly moved it up my spine. I felt power go through me. The pain was gone. Gently he raised me to an upright position and I could look into his face. "Daughter of Sarah and Abraham," he said, "you are set free of your ailment." It was true.

How could I keep from singing? The music poured out of me as I sang about our God

> who forgives all your iniquity,
> who heals all your diseases,
> who redeems your life from the Pit,
> who crowns you with steadfast love and mercy,
> who satisfies you with good as long as you live
> so that your youth is renewed like the eagle's.
>
> —PSALM 103:3–5

The leader of the synagogue was beside himself with rage. He shouted at me, "There are six days to work. Come on those days to be healed, not on the Sabbath."

The rabbi's powerful voice stopped him. "You hypocrite," he said, "you give your ox and donkey water on the Sabbath. The Sabbath is a day of rest given to us so that we may praise God. How could this woman praise God, bent over and in pain? She is healed now so that she can praise God on this very Sabbath. Didn't you hear her singing her love and thanksgiving to God?"

The leader fell silent. Someone began another song and we all joined in:

> Where can I go from your spirit?
> Or where can I flee from your presence?
> If I ascend to heaven, you are there;

if I make my bed in Sheol, you are there.
If I take the wings of the morning
and settle at the farthest limits of the sea,
even there your hand shall lead me,
and your right hand shall hold me fast.
If I say, "Surely the darkness shall cover me,
and the light around me become night,"
even the darkness is not dark to you;
the night is as bright as the day,
for darkness is as light to you.

—PSALM 139:7–12

We sang song after song, and finally the leader of the synagogue gave up and joined in the singing also. When things
quieted down, the rabbi asked, "What is the community of
God like?" Then he said,

It is like a mustard seed that this daughter of Abraham took
and sowed in the garden; it grew and became a tree, and the
birds of the air made nests in its branches.

And again, it is like the yeast that this daughter of Sarah
took and mixed in with three measures of flour until all of it
was leavened, so she made bread for the family. (See Luke
13:18–21.)

Now people crowded around me, happy that I had been
healed. It was a gift to look into their faces again. I had a great
sense of strength, and also wonder. Had not the rabbi called
me "daughter of Sarah and Abraham"? I too am part of God's
community!

Now I teach my granddaughter the songs my grandmother
taught me, and she sings along in her lovely high-pitched voice
as we work in the garden. And from time to time I bend over,
so that she can look into my face and see how much I love her.
And oh, what joy it is to stand up straight again!

Comments

It seemed natural to me to make this a multigenerational story, for rheumatoid arthritis runs in families. My grandmother, who lived with us when I was a child, was a bent-over woman. My mother escaped, but her sister became another bent-over woman. In my generation a cousin has had severe arthritis, but medical science has kept her from being bent over. Even so, I know the pain has often been difficult for her, although she has led an active, normal life.

At a theological conference of Quaker women at Wood-brooke College in Birmingham, England, in 1990, we explored this story. We all practiced walking bent over and made note of what we could see. Indoors we saw the state of the carpet. Outside we saw grass, anthills, and litter. We learned to recognize one another's feet. Hearing became more acute. This story came alive for us.

It seems almost incredible that Jesus would call the woman to come to him in the men's section. The King James Version says, "He called her to him." The Jerusalem and New Revised Standard Versions say, "He called her over." The Revised Standard, J. B. Phillips, and New English Bible all merely say, "He called her." Strong's Exhaustive Concordance breaks the Greek word *prosphoneo* into its root parts: *pros* meaning "toward," and *phoneo* meaning "to address in words or by name." It gives three possible translations for the word: to address, to exclaim, to summon (call unto).

I could not resist the dramatic possibilities of Jesus' calling the woman to him. It would have been shocking to those present. Only the authoritative presence of Jesus could have carried it off. But why would he do it? I speculate that he had sized up the leader of the synagogue in advance as a hypocrite and wished to do something outrageous to break through his facade. Even so, he still felt the need to address him as "you hypocrite."

In these stories we see Jesus breaking many of the taboos against women of his day. This is another case. He must have realized that "separate but not equal" space in the synagogue is oppressive to women. By identifying her as "daughter of Abraham," he gives her full membership in the community of God. Other women present must also have felt a sense of worth and identity.

Reflections

1. Have you had a special relationship with a grandparent? What did this relationship give you that you did not get from your parents or siblings?

2. Was your mother or your grandmother a bent-over woman? Are you? What caused this condition—hard work, perhaps working in the fields? arthritis? osteoporosis? What does modern medicine offer us to alleviate such problems?

3. We have noted various ways of translating the word Jesus used in speaking to the woman. Do you think he really called her into the men's section? Why would he have done so? Why didn't he go to her?

4. Why do you think healing was considered inappropriate for the Sabbath?

5. Some of us grew up in very Sabbath-observing families: no card playing, no movies, etc., just quiet activities like reading, letter-writing, or walks. What do you think Jesus would have thought of such observance of the Sabbath?

6. What do you think of our present "business as usual" on the Sabbath?

CHAPTER 9

Martha

Luke 10:38–42

🌱

Now as they went on their way, he entered a certain village, where a woman named Martha welcomed him into her home.

—LUKE 10:38

Martha's Story

I awoke this morning with a great sense of gratitude. Lazarus has survived one more bout with the demon that possesses him from time to time. Sometimes he is unconscious for so long that we are afraid he may not survive. This bout is over now. I could hear his regular breathing as he slept and knew that when he woke he would be himself again.

I lay there and thought of my family with love and appreciation. We're an odd group: two older unmarried women and their unmarried brother. There is another family member, not related by blood, who is with us when he is in Judea. He comes, but not to stay. Yet he is at the center of all our lives.

I am the eldest. I was five when Lazarus was born. Mother had a hard time at this birth and never did regain her strength. Lazarus was a sickly baby, and we were always afraid we might lose him. Mother could not work hard, so I took over some of the household chores under her direction. I cleaned and cooked and worked in the garden when I had time. Mother did the

spinning and weaving and made clothes for us all. Father usually went for the water each morning and shopped on market
days. He worked in the garden when he was able. However, at
times a demon possessed him and he could not work. Doctors
had not been able to heal him.

Mary was born when I was ten. Mother lingered a few
months; then she died and we buried her in the cave in the
garden. Now all the work fell to me. I never had time to be
with girls my own age. I don't remember ever feeling carefree
or even happy. I worked all day long and still there were more
things that needed doing. Even so, I was glad that Father did
not take another wife, so I did not complain.

Lazarus went to the synagogue school and learned to read
and write. He could recite long passages of scripture and explain what they meant. He wanted to teach me what he was
learning, but I felt I could not take the time. When Mary was
quite young, he began teaching her. She kept up with him and
learned eagerly. I tried not to envy her.

Sometimes demons run in families. Lazarus was about three
when he had the first seizure like Father's. After Mother's death,
Father's spells grew more frequent and intense. He was afraid
he might not live long, so he sent for men from the synagogue
to witness his intentions. The house and grounds were to be
mine, and I was to have full responsibility for Lazarus and Mary.
Father left money with the men to give to us as we needed it.

The men thought Father should arrange a marriage for me,
but he said he would wait. I was carrying a heavy load and was
not yet a woman. He never got around to it, and I was glad.
Now I'm much too old for marriage. Lazarus feels he should
not marry because of the demon. And Mary loves someone
she cannot marry. So here we are.

Lazarus is a wonderful brother. When he is well, he milks
the goat and goes for water each day. He was apprenticed to a
carpenter when he was young and has made shelves to store
things and a little stool for me to stand on to reach the highest
ones. He keeps everything in good repair. He always tells me

how good my goat's milk curds are, and he likes the way I fix the beans. He often tells me how much he loves me and appreciates how well I manage. He even thinks I am still beautiful.

When we were younger, Lazarus often served as a buffer between Mary and me, loving us both and understanding how difficult life has been for both of us. Mary was a very rebellious little girl. She thought I was bossy. She told me I was no fun to be with because I always tried to get her to help with the work. She would say she did not feel well, and while I felt she exaggerated, I never dared push her too much lest she be really ill. If I tried to insist, she would cry and shout, "You can't make me. You're not my mother." In the end I would give in but let my resentment show. Lazarus would take her out to the garden and let her pour out her grievances against me until they were out of her system. Then he would try to help more. I worried that he would overdo. I worried about Mary, too, because I did not know how to reach her.

Father died in the spring, and the men from the synagogue helped us bury him in the cave beside Mother. Mary thought this might not be death but a prolonged bout with the demon. If he did revive, she wanted him to be able to walk out of the cave. She insisted that we wrap each leg separately instead of binding them together as is usually done. The synagogue men finally gave in to her. She did not want the stone rolled across the entry. After four days we all smelled the decay of death. Now Mary gave way to grief and we could not comfort her. We too were deep in our own grief for Father.

Father's death came shortly before the Passover, when Lazarus was twelve. They had planned to go together to the Temple in Jerusalem for the ceremony that would mark Lazarus' reaching manhood. Now he did not want to go without Father. I urged him to find someone else to go with him, but he shook his head and I did not insist.

As I lay in bed remembering all this, I heard Lazarus stir, and I got up to fix breakfast for the two of us. Mary always sleeps late. Lazarus and I began to remember how we first met Jesus, the other member of the family.

Jewish men are obligated to celebrate the Passover in Jerusalem each year, if they can. They stream into the city, often with their families, and the population of the city swells for that week to three times its normal size. Those from Galilee come down the main road along the Jordan River, which then joins the Jericho Road. We live in Bethany, the last stop before Jerusalem. Our house is actually on the Jericho Road. When pilgrims get here, they know they have only two miles left to the Golden Gate into the city.

Lazarus recalled how he and Mary sat in the garden that year, watching the endless procession of pilgrims. I remembered that I took my mending and joined them. It was too hot to work inside. The tramping feet raised the dust and made it seem hotter. A woman fainted not far from our gate, and Lazarus and Mary rushed out to help. They invited the woman's husband to carry her into our garden. Mary fanned her and I brought water, and soon she regained consciousness. They decided to rest for a while before going into the city.

The travelers were Joseph and Mary and their son Jesus from Nazareth in Galilee. We told them our names. Our Mary was excited that she and the mother had the same name. Jesus was an unusual young man, rather tall, with curly hair and a beautiful, serious face. He looked directly at you when you spoke to him, listening intently, giving you his full attention as though what you had to say was important to him.

Like Lazarus, Jesus was twelve and on his way to his first Passover in Jerusalem. When Joseph understood our situation, he invited Lazarus to join them in going to the Temple. In the end we all shared the Passover meal with them in an upper room in the city which they rent each year. Kinspeople of Mary, Elizabeth and her son John, were there too. They live on the other side of Jerusalem, and the Nazareth family spent the rest of the week with them.

Each morning Lazarus met Jesus at the Temple and together they listened to scholars expounding the fine points of the law. Lazarus came home each evening before sundown, his face glowing. He said Jesus asked questions that showed a thorough understanding of the Torah. At times he seemed to know more than the scholar who was speaking.

The week drew to a close. I had invited our friends to share a meal with us before they started back to Galilee. Late in the morning Mary and Joseph came, but Jesus was not with them. He was with friends, they said, and would join them at the place where they planned to camp for the night. Many people from Nazareth camp there. They did not seem concerned about him. Our Mary watched the road all afternoon, sure Jesus would stop to see us on his way north, but he did not come. Lazarus did not watch with her, which surprised me. He seemed subdued and went to bed early. He did not want to talk.

Lazarus was gone when I got up the next morning. Late in the day Mary and Joseph stopped briefly. They had gone from campfire to campfire, but Jesus was not there. They were hurrying back to the city to hunt for him. His mother was beside herself with anxiety. Now I worried about Jesus, and Lazarus too, because he had not come home.

When he returned hours later, I pried out of him what he knew. He said that Jesus felt that God had some great mission for him which he could not pursue in Nazareth. "Can anything good come out of Nazareth?" he asked. His future lay in Jerusalem. Surely one of the scholars would take him on as a scribe. Lazarus urged him to come back to Bethany, but Jesus felt he belonged in Jerusalem.

Lazarus could not sleep. Just before it began to get light he took some food and went into the city. He found Jesus on the steps of the outer court of the Temple, leaning against a pillar, asleep. He was disheveled, and his tunic badly rumpled and torn. He told Lazarus that before sundown everyone had left the Temple. No one invited him home as he had hoped might happen. A priest gave him some meat from the altar. When

Jesus tried to eat it, beggars lurking in the shadows snatched it from him. They searched him roughly, finding a small bag of coins which they divided among themselves. Jesus took the food Lazarus had brought and ate it ravenously. Lazarus insisted they exchange tunics. He brought home the one Jesus had been wearing so that I could wash and mend it.

Another night passed. Then about noon Jesus and his parents stopped at our house. Jesus and Lazarus went off by themselves while I fixed food for the travelers. Later Lazarus told us what they had talked about. Jesus had confided in Lazarus that he saw no way out but to go home with his parents and, as he put it, *be subject to them* for the time being. He felt his mother did not really understand that he was a man now, and able to look out for himself. My heart ached for all of them when I heard this. After they had eaten they took leave of us and said they would see us at the next Passover.

We watched as they started out. Then Jesus came running back to us, a bit out of breath. "Martha, Mary, Lazarus," he said, "I need a home near Jerusalem. I need a Judean family." We embraced him and told him that our home was his now and that we were all happy to have him part of our family.

He lingered a moment at the gate, the sun illuminating his beautiful head. I caught my breath. This is how the Messiah will look when he comes, I thought. And deep within me, I *knew*, even then: He really was God's chosen one. I kept this knowledge in my heart, and did not tell Mary or Lazarus. The certainty grew with each passing year. Now I told Lazarus. He nodded, and we sat there quietly holding hands. We never know when he will come, nor how long he will stay, but his room is always ready for him.

Now we heard Mary stirring. She came down from sleeping on the roof and took the pitcher to get water. After Jesus became part of the family, I learned not to nag her and she learned to offer to help.

When she finished breakfast, I decided to air the bedding and wash the clothes. It was a beautiful day. I would get a head start on the annual cleaning before the Passover. I felt full of energy. Jesus usually came for the Festival of Unleavened Bread, but that was still a month away. This year, with the work done, I would be free to enjoy his visit. The day wore on. The house became clean, and I became dirty. I thought longingly of a bath and clean clothes.

I was just finishing the last task when Lazarus called, "Martha, Jesus is here." There were people with him, but he sent them on ahead. Lazarus and Mary ran up to greet him, but I felt too grubby to embrace him. Then I saw that he was also grubby from the journey. Mary ran for water and began to wash his feet. Lazarus brought clean clothes, and I gave him a drink of cold water. He sat down under a tree and Mary curled up at his feet.

I gathered beans and a cucumber, and found a melon just at its peak. I carried them into the kitchen and started a fire. The heat was oppressive. I was very tired. I could hear the three of them talking in the cool of the garden. Once again I resented the fact that Mary thought she could join the men, exempt from kitchen drudgery. Then everything went wrong. The fire was too hot and the beans burned. The knife slipped and I cut my hand as I sliced the cucumber. Blood ran down on the slices. I called Mary to come and help, but she pretended not to hear. I began to cry.

I went to the doorway and asked, "Jesus, don't you care that my sister has left me all alone to do the work? Tell her to help me." Surely he would take my side. But no! His reply stung me. "Martha, Martha," he said, "you are worried and distracted by many things. There is need of only one thing. Mary has chosen the better part which will not be taken away from her."

Lazarus came and led me to the cool place under the tree and helped me sit down. I said stubbornly, "How can a woman show her welcome to someone she loves except by preparing a good meal?" Jesus was silent for a moment. Then he said that hospitality is not always food and a clean house, nice as those things are. Hospitality, he went on, is being willing to pay attention to a guest, to listen attentively to what is on the guest's mind.[1]

He said he had felt he must return to Jerusalem, to teach and preach in Judea for a time. It might mean confrontation with authorities. It might mean his arrest. It might even mean his death. He wanted to lay all this before us, so that we would understand and could help and support him. He said we are important to him; we are his family. Some of his followers who travel with him do not understand his mission yet. They still expect him to lead a revolt against the Romans. We listened; we asked questions to understand better; and we promised him our steadfast love and support.

We talked long into the evening. The sun went down and stars came out. Then we sat in silence, bound together by our love for one another. Finally Lazarus said, "I'm hungry for cold, burned beans and bloodstained cucumber slices, and I think I saw a melon." We went into the kitchen and Lazarus lit the lamp. The food tasted so good!

Now at the end of this long day, I am lying in my bed again, remembering all that has happened. I pray that I may let go of all the mundane concerns that distract me and that I may be worthy of Jesus' trust and love and be strong for the fateful days ahead. I pray that I may always give my full attention to this great *guest of my life*.[2]

Comments

The Gospels give three stories about Mary and Martha: the brief one in Luke, which is the basis for this portrait of Martha, and two longer ones in John, on which chapter 13, Mary's chapter, is based.

I have added three things from John's stories to help fill out Luke's scanty tale. First, Martha and Mary have a brother, Lazarus. Second, they live in Bethany, which John tells us is about two miles from Jerusalem. It is a small town on the lower slopes of the Mount of Olives. And third, Jesus loves them dearly, and they love him. John seems to imply a long, close friendship. In John 11:5 we read, "Jesus loved Martha and her sister and Lazarus."

When the sisters send Jesus a message that Lazarus needs healing, they say, "He whom you love is ill" (John 11:3). One might ask whether Lazarus is "the disciple Jesus loved."

When you try to outline Luke's Gospel historically, this story is clearly part of Jesus' journey from Galilee to Jerusalem. In Luke 9, which precedes this story, Luke writes that Jesus set his face to go to Jerusalem, and begins this story with the words, "Now as they went on their way, he entered a certain village, where a woman named Martha welcomed him into her home."

Luke's story, only five verses long, presents a number of problematic circumstances for which I have tried to account:

1. Luke clearly says that the house is Martha's. Women could inherit only if they had no brothers. If Lazarus was there, why isn't this his house? Further, why are two apparently unmarried sisters living together? Their father should have arranged marriages for them, or their brother if the father is no longer living. I have tried to account for these two anomalies by giving Lazarus a serious, recurring, hereditary illness. The father dies early and arranges that Martha, the eldest, shall be in charge of her siblings, and that it shall be her house, since Lazarus at times cannot function and may die early. John indicates that the family had its own tomb, suggesting a measure of prosperity, which I have implied, but not accounted for.

2. The two women seem immature. Martha appears to be an incompetent housewife who cannot get a meal on the table by herself. Mary comes across as a spoiled brat who will not help. I have found mitigating circumstances for Martha in this story. Mary's story comes later in this book (chapter 13).

3. I have wrestled, as many women have over the centuries, with Jesus' seeming rebuke of Martha. It seems a real breach

of etiquette on a guest's part to criticize someone struggling to get a meal for you. Then to take the lazy sister's part seems unusually insensitive and cruel. (In Luke 7:44–46, Jesus rebukes his host, Simon, for *not* providing all the niceties of hospitality. Is there no pleasing him?)

The only way I can make sense of this story is in the context of a long, intimate friendship, even a family relationship, in which people are so close that they speak their minds freely without weighing their words. Misunderstandings are cleared up without permanent hurts. But how could three people in Bethany have such a close relationship with someone living several days' journey north in Galilee?

This sent me back to the Gospels to hunt for something that might have triggered such a relationship. I studied the location of Bethany, on the Jericho Road, two miles from Jerusalem. Jesus and his family might well have passed Martha's house on their way to the Passover when he was twelve.

The story of Jesus in the Temple, talking to the scholars at age twelve, ought to have come early in this book. But the only woman mentioned in the story is his mother, and it is much too soon to include her story, because so much more happens between them. I reluctantly left out the incident when he was twelve.

The possibility grew of making that Passover the beginning of the long, close relationship with the Bethany family, and including it as a flashback in Martha's story. The more I lived with this possibility, the more the two stories came together as they now appear in this chapter. Reader reaction will have to tell me whether this is convincing.

For the picture of Jesus sitting forlornly on the steps of the Temple after trying to make it on his own in Jerusalem, I am indebted to an unpublished short story called "Mary's Side of the Story," by McGregor Gray of Brunswick, Maine, an associate of the Jesus Seminar.

Reflections

1. Luke says that "a woman named Martha welcomed Jesus into her home," indicating that the house belonged not to Lazarus, the male heir, but to Martha. Do you think the explanation for this in the story is plausible? Can you think of other possibilities?

2. Did you ever feel that you were always stuck in the kitchen, or at some dull chore, while others relaxed near by and did not offer to help? How did you deal with the situation?

3. How important is it for you to have a clean house and a well-prepared meal for guests? Does it bother you to have people drop in when the house is a mess? and to have them tarry until mealtime? Can you comfortably invite them to help improvise a meal?

4. Some women feel that this story puts them down for accepting the role into which a male-oriented society has placed them. If you are a woman, how have you felt about this story? How do you feel about it, if you are a man?

5. Have you known women who boldly refused to be stuck in the kitchen, and took part in interesting conversations while others did the work? If you are a woman, how do you feel about such women? If you are a man, how do you feel?

6. Do you feel that Martha deserved to be rebuked?

7. How do you personally make sense out of this brief, fragmentary story? Is the explanation given in this story plausible? Does the flashback to the Passover when Jesus was twelve work?

CHAPTER 10

The Woman Who Anointed Jesus

Mark 14:1–9

> It was two days before the Passover and the festival of Unleavened Bread. The chief priests and the scribes were looking for a way to arrest Jesus by stealth and kill him. . . . While he was at Bethany in the house of Simon the leper, as he sat at the table, a woman came with an alabaster jar of very costly ointment of nard, and she broke open the jar and poured the ointment on his head.
>
> —MARK 14:1, 3

The Story of the Woman Who Anointed Jesus

I saw what was going to happen. The priests and Pharisees were jealous of him. He knew the scriptures thoroughly, better than most of them. They feared his healing power and the great crowds that followed him everywhere. I saw them watching him in the Temple, and I knew that they would not rest until they had done away with him. They would move against him very soon. I knew also that Jesus would not compromise for his own safety.

Does no one know who he is? Am I the only one alive who remembers that this man of the house and lineage of David was born to be king? That it was all foretold in the stars at the time of his birth? Oh, I knew from the beginning that he would not drive out the Romans and set himself up as a temporal ruler. He was born for greater things. I watched him cast himself in the role of servant, and at the same time heard him say that the servant of all would be the greatest among them. Would he now go to his death without ever having been recognized, anointed, and consecrated king?

I remembered how Samuel had been told to go to Jesse and anoint one of his sons king. Jesse had brought out seven sons, and each time God said to Samuel, "No, not this one." Then under Samuel's pressure Jesse had finally sent for his youngest son, a shepherd, and it is written:

> Now [David] was ruddy, and had beautiful eyes, and was handsome. God said "Rise and anoint him, for this is the one." Then Samuel took the horn of oil, and anointed him in the presence of his brothers; and the spirit of God came mightily upon David from that day forward. (1 Sam. 16:12–13)

And I thought, Jesus too is handsome, and has beautiful eyes . . . And oh, how the spirit of God has come mightily upon this descendant of David!

I thought of the men among his disciples, all afraid for their lives now. None of them would anoint him, certainly not at my asking. I believed that this symbolic act would comfort him, would consecrate his death and give him strength to face it. So, although no king of Israel has ever been anointed by a woman, I had to do it. I had no choice.

How long have I carried this knowledge in my heart? For at least thirty years it has never been out of my mind. Perhaps I should tell you my story, so that you will understand why I feel so strongly about his being anointed.

My mother died giving me birth, and I grew up with my grandmother. She was known as "the crone," as I am today. We lived in her small hut in the hills near Bethlehem. I early learned from her the various herbs for healing, when to harvest them, and how to dry and preserve them. Even when I was small, she took me with her to deliver babies, for she had no one with whom to leave me. By the time I was ten, I had delivered a child myself.

She also taught me to read the heavens and to foretell events from the position of the planets and constellations. She was a night person, as I am. Many evenings we climbed the hill near our hut to watch the stars come into view on the horizon and slowly move across the sky. Sometimes we watched until dawn turned the eastern sky faintly pink. Then we went home to sleep away the heat of the day.

You may think it a strange girlhood. I had no friends my own age. I did not run and play as children do. I loved my grandmother and eagerly learned all she could teach me. Early in my life I knew that I shared her gift of healing. And I have her gift of prophecy, too, and of seeing the deeper meaning of things.

Before she died, my grandmother took me once more to the lean-to shed by our house where she kept her supplies. She had me go over all the herbs and ointments until she was satisfied that I really knew them as well as she did. "Now I can die in peace," she said. I live now as she lived, in the same little hut. I gather my herbs in their season. People know me and trust me and send for me when I am needed.

I continue to watch the heavens for signs. I know the waxing and the waning of the moon. I follow the movement of the planets. I know when they will move close to each other and there will be a conjunction. Every twenty years there is a conjunction of Jupiter and Saturn. I have seen it three times now, the first time with my grandmother.

She told me of a time when Jupiter and Saturn would be opposite the sun, from our point of view on earth. This time, she said, there would be a triple conjunction, that is, the two planets would move close to each other three times within a few months. They would not meld into a single point of light, she said, but would be close enough to illuminate the whole night sky.

She did not live to see that, but I watched for it. This time the conjunction took place in the constellation Pisces. I was greatly excited, for Pisces is associated with our people, and Jupiter is a sign of a world ruler. Someone of great importance to the whole world was about to be born right here among us.

Days passed, and the second conjunction took place. This time the whole sky was bright and the two planets seemed to be shining right over our little town of Bethlehem. In great excitement I left the hill and made my way to the village. The dark streets of Bethlehem were bright tonight. I walked to the center of town where the inn is, not knowing where to go, but knowing I must go.

I met the innkeeper's wife coming out the door with her cloak on. She rushed up when she saw me. She had been starting out to find me, she said. Earlier in the evening her husband had had to turn away a couple because there was no room for them at the inn. He had offered them shelter in a cave behind the inn, used as a stable. The woman was going to have a baby and now her labor had begun.

I always go prepared with packets of herbs and little jars of ointment tucked into my belt. I never know when I may be needed. I sent the innkeeper's wife back for hot water and clean linen as I hurried to the cave. The man was distraught because his wife was in great pain. She thanked me for coming so quickly. I gave her something to ease the pain, and when the hot water came, I made a potion to hasten her contractions.

So I was there to help his mother bring him into the world. I held him as he drew his first breaths. What a beautiful child! He was ruddy, and when he opened his eyes, I saw that they were beautiful, too. He might have been David's son. I asked the man why they were on the road with the birth so near. He said he had to come to Bethlehem for the enrollment for taxes that the emperor had ordered. Because he was of David's lineage, Bethlehem was his place of enrollment. It seemed best that his wife come with him. She hoped the baby might be born in David's city. It all fitted together.

And I thought: how right that a future world leader should be born in a stable, in an occupied country, in a remote corner of the mighty Roman Empire! God works in mysterious ways, exalting the humble.

I went back each day to make sure that mother and child were well. I loved to hold that beautiful baby. The little family had many visitors. Shepherds wandered in, their shaggy dogs quietly watching. People in the town brought food and little gifts for the baby. He did not lack for clothes, thanks to their generosity.

On the twelfth night, the third and final conjunction of Jupiter and Saturn lit up the sky. They seemed to be right over the stable. That night there were visitors who had come a long way, Parthian astrologers who, in Babylon, had seen the first conjunction and had known its meaning. They had set out at once on their camels across the desert to find the new little king. They brought him gifts: resin from the frankincense tree that grows at the southern end of the Arabian peninsula, and resin from the myrrh tree. These are rare and costly gifts. They brought gold also.

They had gone first to Jerusalem, supposing the new king would be born there. They had met Herod, and after talking to him did not trust him. They surmised that he would try to do away with this new little rival. The final conjunction led them to the stable. They came with a warning about Herod. The little family left Bethlehem in haste, hoping to get to Egypt, beyond Herod's reach.

I saw him only occasionally during his early years, but I kept track of the family. When they were in Judea, I tried to be where they were without intruding. I knew when he came for his first Passover in Jerusalem and frightened his family by remaining behind in the Temple, talking to the scholars, while they hunted frantically for him.

I was in the crowd when John baptized him in the Jordan River. When most of the people had dispersed, I went to him and told him that I had brought him into the world. He said his mother had told him of me. We talked, and I asked about his plans. He said he would reject violence and temporal power. He planned to go into the desert for a time, to clarify his mission and his message. It was evident to me that this was no ordinary man. He was full of the spirit of God.

After he returned to Galilee I did not see him often. I had my own people to look after, and they kept me busy. I counted myself his disciple, however. Some are called to travel with him. Others, like the family in Bethany with whom he usually stays when he is in Judea, are called to say home. No one is closer to him than Martha and Mary and their brother, Lazarus. He called women as well as men, and I am glad. I know and love some of them.

Now there is not much time left for him. My grandmother told me of an ancient tradition, older than David, that the true test of rulership is willingness to give up one's life for one's people. A king would know the right time. He was descended from David, but he was also linked to rulers who, before the times of domination and violence, had ruled with love and forbearance, willing to give up their lives for the sake of truth.

I made my preparations. I pulled out from under my straw pallet a small drawstring bag of coins, all the money I had. I counted it carefully. Then I went to the dealer in oils and ointments. I had brought his children into the world and had saved the life of one of his sons when he had a high fever. He greeted me warmly.

I spread out my coins and told him that I needed an aromatic oil, something suitable for an anointing. He brought out several bottles, but none seemed right. He saw my disappointment and asked if it was for someone important. I nodded. He hesitated a moment and then brought out a small, very beautiful alabaster bottle. It was sealed, but even so I was aware of a faint and lovely odor. He said it was oil of spikenard, which grows high in the mountains of India. I knew it was right, but I also knew that my small store of coins would not buy it. I hesitated. Then he said impulsively, "Take it!" He added that it was fit to anoint a high priest, or even a king. I bowed to him and thanked him humbly.

I made my way to Bethany and went to Martha's house, where his friends often gather. I learned that he would have dinner the next night with Simon, who also lived in Bethany. Jesus had healed him of leprosy. The men of Jesus' inner circle were also among the invited guests.

The next night I stood inconspicuously near Simon's house, my precious little bottle in my hand. Finally he and his friends gathered and went into the house. When they were all there, I went in quietly. I waited a moment and then went to where Jesus lay on his couch at the low table. I broke the seal on the bottle and poured the fragrant oil on his beautiful head and laid my hands on him in blessing. The lovely odor filled the room and drew all eyes to what I was doing. Thus I anointed him king in the presence of his friends.

I had supposed they would recognize this as a holy act. But no! I had not realized how discouraged and frightened and confused they were. Someone said pettishly, "What is the use of wasting that? The oil could have been sold and the money given to the poor." Others took up the complaint. They were angry at what I had done.

Jesus' voice rang out, silencing them. "Leave her alone," he said. "She has done a beautiful thing." He said they could help the poor any time, but he would not be with them much longer. He went on more quietly, "She has done what she could; she has anointed my body beforehand for its burial. Truly I tell you, wherever the good news is proclaimed in the whole world, what she has done will be told in remembrance of her."

And not one of them there, except Jesus, knew my name!

My heart ached for him. I left quietly. I thought of the narrow-mindedness of those who see life in terms of money. I grieve for those who never make an extravagant gesture, never spend all they have to give a luxurious gift to someone they love, never pour out the whole contents of the bottles of their lives in devotion. I heard Jesus say once that the community of God is like a buyer looking for fine pearls. When he finds an unusually beautiful one, he sells everything he has to buy it. O ye blind and greedy of heart, life is meant to be spent!

I walked back to Martha's house and found many of the women gathered there. I greeted them all. There were the Marys: Jesus' mother, and Martha's sister, and of course, the one from Magdala, and the one married to Clopas. Joanna and Susanna were there too, and that refreshingly outspoken woman who is the mother of James and John, two of the first disciples. And many others.

I told them what had happened. They understood, and I was comforted. They will not desert him, whatever happens. They will be with him until the end, and beyond that. They will keep his message alive so that it will not perish from the earth.

I will stay in Jerusalem until what is to be has come to be. Then I will go home and once again serve my people. And I will climb my hill at night, watching the stars and the planets and the phases of the moon.

I know that his story will be told as long as the earth endures. So I have told my story, in memory of him.

Comments

All four Gospels record anointing stories. John writes that Jesus was a guest of Lazarus in Bethany. Martha served the dinner and Mary anointed his feet. Apparently the women kept their familiar roles. (See John 12:1–8.)

Luke sets his story in the beginning of Jesus' ministry, before he goes to Galilee. Here he is the guest of Simon, a Pharisee. Luke's anointer is "a woman in the city, who was a sinner." She too anoints his feet, an act of hospitality in a time when people walked everywhere and were likely to have dirty, aching feet when they arrived as guests. (See Luke 7:30–50.)

Matthew and Mark tell virtually the same story. I decided to use Mark's, since it is the older of the two, but have included a few details from Matthew. (See Matthew 16:6–13.)

In her book *In Memory of Her,* Elisabeth Schüssler Fiorenza made me aware that the anointing of the head was not a routine act of hospitality, like washing the feet, but rather a symbolic act, the recognition of a king.[1]

Elisabeth Moltmann-Wendel carried my thinking one step further in her book *The Women around Jesus.* She suggests that the woman may have been a wise woman, one who knows the future and can see things clearly.[2]

Starhawk's book *The Spiral Dance* suggested to me that the test of great rulership is the willingness to give up one's life for one's people.[3]

As I began working on this story, I thought of the woman as living near Bethany, where the story takes place. Then a member of the Friends Meeting in Helena, Montana, an amateur astronomer who writes under the name Starshine, told me of her research into the scientific and historic basis for the star of Bethlehem. This seemed to supply a missing element in the story. The anointer lived near Bethlehem, rather than Bethany, and was accustomed to watching the night sky. She had witnessed the conjunction and had known its meaning. After reading Moltmann-Wendel, I was already quite sure she was a healer. Now it seemed possible that she had been the midwife at the birth of Jesus. The details of the story fell rapidly into place and it seemed to write itself, as if this unknown woman were really telling me her story.

Reflections

1. What does the symbol of anointing mean to us today? What kinds of anointing have you witnessed?
2. The woman in the story given here seems to have something in common with women who were persecuted as

witches in the seventeenth century. Is it reasonable to believe there have been such women in every century? Have
you known women who had healing power and who were
able to see into the future? How have they been treated?

3. Why do you think the men felt the need to put her down?

4. Have you ever bought a "pearl of great price"? Was it worth
the expenditure of all that you had?

5. When David in the heat of battle expressed a wish for a
drink from the well at Bethlehem, not really expecting it,
some of his men risked their lives to go through enemy lines
to get it for him. David was very much moved by their devotion and love and courage, but he could not drink the water, and poured it out on the ground. Have you ever been
the recipient of an expensive gift that you knew the giver
could not afford? Did you feel you could accept it?

6. In this story, has the author taken too many liberties with
the Gospel account?

CHAPTER 11

Mary Magdalene

Luke 8:1–3, 24:1–11; Mark 15:40–41, 16:1–11;
Matthew 27:55–56, 28:1–10; John 19:25, 20:1–18

❧

Soon afterwards he went on through cities and villages,
proclaiming and bringing the good news. . . . The twelve
were with him, as well as some women who had been cured
of evil spirits and infirmities: Mary, called Magdalene, from
whom seven demons had gone out, . . . and many others.

—LUKE 8:1–3a

Mary Magdalene's Story

I was seventeen that summer, and I wished I had never been
born. Every other girl my age in Magdala was married and
most had several children. I was still living at home, and I saw
no way of leaving my father's house. Every day he reminded
me that he had been unable to find a husband for me. No one
wanted me at any price, he said.

You see, from time to time a demon possessed me. My
muscles would suddenly contract and I would lose consciousness and fall to the ground, thrashing wildly. In a little while I
would come to myself. No one ever helped me as I struggled
to get up from the ground. Grown people avoided me. Children pointed at me and chanted, "devil's child." Sometimes
they imitated my seizures and laughed hilariously. I was angry
at them. I was angry at the indifferent adults. I was angry at
myself, because no matter how hard I tried, I could not stop
the seizures. I had to suppress the rage I felt at my father, who

blamed me for something I could not help. I was afraid to be angry with God, but that resentment was there too, just below the surface of my life.

My mother loved me and did not blame me for my affliction, but she did insist that I must do my share of the work. Part of that was going to the village well every day for water. It was a nightmare. I usually got to the well with no problem. I lowered my pitcher and drew it up, but on the way back, the demon often hurled me to the ground. The water spilled, drenching me, and sometimes the pitcher broke. Then I would have to start over.

The older I grew, the more frequent the seizures seemed to be. I tried not to think about it when I started for the well, but fear would creep in as I saw people turn away to avoid me, and children watching in the distance, hoping that I would put on a scene for them. The harder I tried to ignore them, the more likely it was that the demon would take over my body. I asked my mother to let me do something else instead, but she felt it was important for me to try to overcome my demon. Life did not seem worth living. I saw no hope for the future. None of the physicians my parents had consulted had been able to help me.

Magdala is a village on the west side of the Sea of Galilee, between Capernaum on the north and Tiberias, the city that grew up around Herod's new summer palace, on the south. Its steep streets slope down to the water, and its whitewashed houses look down over the roofs of other houses to the Sea of Galilee.

My father was a fisherman, in business with my two older brothers. They were both married and lived near us. Much of the year, the men fish at night when the catch is larger. Except in really cold weather, I slept on the roof. When I woke in the morning, I could look down over the roofs to the water, and usually I could see my father's boat. When I saw that he had turned back to shore, ready to sell the night's catch to the fish dealer, I went down to help my mother prepare breakfast for him.

Sometimes Father picked up news on the way home. As he ate, he would tell us what was going on in Magdala and the other seacoast towns. One morning he said that a new rabbi had come to Capernaum and taken a little house on the edge of town. He apparently went out on preaching missions to neighboring villages. People said he had the gift of healing. A small hope began to grow inside me. I wondered how I might meet him. Father said that this man had approached some of the Capernaum fishermen and four of them had actually left their boats to join him. Father said he hoped the rabbi would not come to Magdala, but if he did, Father would keep a close watch on my brothers so they would not be bewitched like the Capernaum men.

Several mornings later I looked down at the shore when I woke and saw a group around a fire, apparently preparing food. There were a half dozen men and a woman or two. When my father and brothers pulled their boats out of the water, a man left the group around the fire and came up to Father to buy fish. He apparently said something else, for Father shook his head vigorously, motioned to my brothers to follow him, and stalked away.

The man turned back to the fire. To my astonishment, he looked up and saw me and waved. And before I could think, I waved back. Then I was ashamed. What kind of man would wave at a woman he had not met, and what kind of woman was I to respond? If this was the rabbi Father had told us of, what kind of women would follow him and his male disciples? I thought the worst of the whole group.

And so did Father as he stumped into the house. I brought water and washed his feet. He told how the man had bought fish and then invited my brothers and him to have breakfast with them. Father said he told him to get out of town and leave decent, hardworking men alone.

Father finished his meal and went off to sleep. Mother and I cleared away the food. It was time for me to go for water, so I took my pitcher and left. At the well I found the same group of people I had seen having breakfast on the shore. No one else was in sight. The two women stood a little apart and I looked at them curiously. They were not what I expected. They were neatly and modestly dressed and, to my small-town eyes, full of dignity. The only women I knew were like my mother. They loved their families, but they gossiped and complained when they met at the well. Their interests were limited to housework, children, and how to manipulate their husbands. In contrast, these women seemed to have a sense of themselves that I had never seen in the women of the town and did not understand.

The men were sitting on the curbing of the well, and their leader looked up as I came. I stared at him. I had never seen anyone like him. He seemed full of—what shall I say?—*grace* was the word that came to me. Rising to greet me, he told me that his name is Jesus.

They had broken their pitcher. He asked if they might each have a drink when I drew up mine. It was the first time a man I did not know had ever spoken to me, but it seemed the natural thing for him to do. I nodded and let my pitcher down. I drew it up and turned to hold it for him to drink first.

And then, of course, it happened! I lost consciousness and the water spilled, soaking my clothes. He apparently stooped down and touched me on the shoulder and I regained consciousness. I heard him speak sharply to the demon, "Come out of her and never trouble her again." He helped me to my feet and I stammered my thanks. I let the pitcher down again and this time there was no disaster.

While they drank, Jesus said to me, "Would you like to be whole?" "Oh sir," I said, "more than anything in the world." He told me that I need never have another seizure if I had faith in my own wholeness. He added that I had other demons that only I could exorcise. Seeing that I did not understand, he explained that he saw I carried anger and bitterness within me, as well as self-pity and rejection of other people, hopelessness, and lack of joy. He had really described me quite accurately, I had to admit.

Looking at him and at the two women, I began to see what wholeness might mean. "Sir," I said, "I do want to be whole, and I will work at getting rid of all my demons." Then, without thinking, I blurted out, "Will you help me? Will you be my teacher?" I realized that I had asked for something that women are forbidden to have. He was silent so long that I was afraid I had offended him. Then he said, "Will you follow me?"

I asked if he meant that I should join the group. He told me to think about it and to be sure that I was ready to leave home and family. He said that they would be in Magdala for two more days. If I wanted to join them, I should be there at dawn at the well, on the third day. He said they would come back to Magdala again, from time to time, and I could leave the group if it did not work out. I didn't think my father would ever take me back. And I thought, What is there to look forward to in Magdala?

He called the two women over and introduced them. Susanna is a widow who had lived in poverty and hopelessness until Jesus called her. Salome had left an abusive husband who blamed her for being barren. They told me of their new life with Jesus and said that they were truly happy for the first time in their lives. I wanted to join them.

I saw my mother coming, and knew she must have worried at my long absence. I told her I was really healed, that the demon would never come back. I introduced her to Susanna and Salome, and they told her how their lives had changed since they agreed to follow Jesus. They talked about their new life and told my mother that if I did join the group, they would look after me and help me. Now Jesus came and introduced the six men. Simon and Andrew are brothers, as are James and John. They are from Capernaum. Philip and Nathaniel are from Bethsaida.

Father was still asleep when we returned home. We did not talk about what had happened for fear of waking him. When he left for the night's fishing, I told Mother every detail. I said I really wanted to join the group.

She agreed to think about it and to say nothing to Father, even about the healing. She had been impressed by the women herself and was not utterly opposed to my joining them. She also said that she too had never met a man like Jesus. He was not at all like the impression of him she'd had from Father.

Very early on the third morning, before Father returned home, I packed a change of clothes in a small bundle which I carried over my shoulder on a stick. Mother gave me a small cloth bag with coins which I tucked into my belt. This was my dowry. I would not be a burden to the group. I knew in my heart that I was leaving my father's house forever, and that meant leaving Mother, too. At that moment I almost changed my mind. Then I kissed her goodbye and turned my face to the future.

Jesus and his friends were there at the well. In the dim light we turned south, walking along the shore. After an hour we came to a small village. Fishing boats were coming in. The men built a fire and Jesus bought fish. Susanna made unleavened bread. How good the food tasted!

So my real life began. Up until now I'd been absorbed with the problem of the demon. Now that was over. It was as if I were seeing everything for the first time. I had never noticed how beautiful the earth is, the grass and flowers, clouds and birds. Everything was a delight to me. We walked south, most of the time by the Sea of Galilee. It was constantly in motion, with the play of light and shadow always shifting into new patterns. Everything seemed new and fresh, as it must have on the day God created the world.

People were beautiful too. Children in towns where we stopped were drawn to Jesus, their faces shining with love. People he healed were full of gratitude and new hope, and their faces shone too. And I had never known men and women like the ones in our group. They had left families, jobs, homes to join him. They believed he was the bearer of God's truth, and they wanted to help spread his message. Their hearts were full of hope for the new community of God of which he talked and wanted to help him bring it into being.

And dominating everything was his intense presence. always seeing the world suffused with the presence of God, always full of new ideas, and telling wonderful stories to make the ideas real and easy to remember. Through it all flowed his sense of God's presence with us, not a God far off and judgmental, but close at hand, so that we all lived in that presence. Like every pious Jewish man, he called God *Abba* (Daddy) when he prayed, and when he used the word it brought God's loving, understanding presence powerfully to us.

My own perception of God grew, too. I lost the inscrutable and punitive deity who had punished me with a demon—for what? My mother was the only one who had had compassion for me. A line from one of David's songs kept running through my head: "My soul is like a weaned child with its mother" (Ps. 131:2). Was God like a mother's lap? Was God everlasting arms holding us tenderly? Later I heard Jesus speak of wanting to gather people together "like a mother hen."

Our days fell into a pleasant rhythm. When we came to a village, we went to the well and Jesus began talking to anyone who was there. Usually a crowd gathered. He told them about the community of God, which is not like the Roman Empire and other kingdoms where rulers lord it over people and push them around. It is a community of friends—the oppressed and the humble, women and children, are all part of it. He told his wonderful stories to make his points. We mingled with people and talked with them too. If we saw people who needed healing, we brought them to Jesus.

Sometimes people invited us to share their food and perhaps let us sleep in their barns. At other times Salome, Susanna, and I bought food at a market or from a farmer's wife. The men made a fire and we cooked supper. After we had eaten, we sat around the fire and talked. I found that I could say what I thought and could express my ideas clearly. Even the men listened to me. This was a new experience for a woman. Later someone banked the fire and we slept, the men on one side of the fire and the women on the other.

In time we came to Tiberias. Near the summer palace on the waterfront is a large market and the well. A crowd gathered quickly when Jesus began to talk. I noticed a well-dressed woman standing somewhat apart from the crowd. She beckoned to me, and when I walked over to her she asked if I was a follower of Jesus. She wanted to know what our life was like, and I told her, not softening the hardships but dwelling on the great joy we all felt. Her name is Joanna. Her husband, who is Herod's steward, had divorced her. She and her maid wished to become followers of Jesus. Mary, the maid, was in the group close to Jesus, waiting for a chance to speak to him. Joanna was afraid that Jesus might turn her away, and I reassured her that that was not likely.

I looked at her beautiful clothes and dainty slippers and suggested we go shopping for new clothes at the market nearby. We found some plainer, sturdier garments, and also substantial sandals to replace her impractical slippers. We found a place where she could change her clothes. She gave her cast-off garments to a beggar woman, who stared at us in disbelief. Then I brought her to Jesus. She told him of her friendship with John the Baptizer and of his awful death. Tears came to Jesus' eyes. He told her that she and Mary were welcome to join our group, but that Mary must no longer be thought of as her maid. She agreed. I know the adjustment must not have been easy for her, but she never looked back. She and Mary became much-loved members of our group.

One night as we lay around the fire, I was unable to sleep. I sat up and looked up into the beautiful night sky, thanking God for my new life. I became aware that on the other side of the fire, Jesus too was awake. Presently he rose and started to walk. He turned and motioned to me to follow him.

We walked for a time in silence, and then he asked how things were going for me. I told him I loved my new life and was at peace. I said that all the women are happy. We are all better off, living our simple, wandering life with him, living out his vision of a community of friends committed to God. The community of God seemed like our own dream of how things should be. He said that some of the men still thought he might raise an army and start a revolution. A few were becoming impatient.

Night after night we walked and talked in this way. I wanted to be the listener he seemed to need, but I soon found that I also had ideas and insights for which he thanked me. I had always called him "teacher," and now he said that I was his teacher also.

I came to love him utterly, body and soul, yet I never wanted more than what I had: to be with him, to share his life, to minister to him in little ways, to listen to him with full attention, and then to talk with him about his ideas and how he could explain them more clearly. I know that I filled his need for someone who fully understood what he was called to do.

One night we talked longer than usual and came back as it was beginning to get light. Simon was awake, warming himself by the fire. He looked up at the two of us in disbelief. He shouted, "Look, Jesus, we have left everything to follow you." Jesus stopped him and said, "If I choose to be with any one of my friends, what is that to you? You are to follow me yourself."

Peter's shouting woke everyone, and now they all knew. The other women accepted my closeness to Jesus, but some of the men resented it. They did not understand why Jesus called women in the first place, although when a meal appeared every night, they were glad enough for our presence. They could not understand why Jesus would want to talk to a woman, much less listen to her opinions. Although most Jewish men thanked God in a daily prayer that they had not been born female, Jesus treated all women as human beings whose friendship was important to him. None of us had ever experienced that kind of friendship from a man before, and we all loved him for it.

Simon Peter was a jealous man. As one of the first Jesus called, he felt he should be closest to him. He and Andrew and their neighbors James and John were all fishermen without much education. Of these, only John really grasped things quickly and understood what Jesus was talking about. This brought John very close to Jesus and love grew between them, so that people sometimes spoke of John as "the disciple Jesus loves." Peter came to resent John, both his closeness to Jesus and his ability to grasp ideas quickly.

And if Peter was jealous of John, how much more was he jealous of me. He talked about me behind my back and started rumors about me. I know that Jesus loved him very much and was sure that in time he would understand everything. And Peter was often lovable. He was enthusiastic, impetuous, and had an engaging grin, like a little boy's. Even when he was being stubborn, he would grin.

Jesus and I continued to walk at night but were careful to wait until Peter was sleeping soundly, and careful to return early. Jesus now began to talk about returning to Jerusalem, and I was filled with fear. I had hoped our present life would never end. But he felt God called him to this, and I saw that he set his face steadfastly to return to Jerusalem. I assured him of my support and told him I would try to help the others understand. I knew that I must not let my love for him stand in the way of his doing what he was called to do, so I did not try to talk him out of returning to the Holy City.

He kept calling more people, both men and women. We were now quite a large group. Now he called everyone together and said that he must return to Jerusalem. We could all go, if we felt called to, but anyone who wished to remain in Galilee was free to do so. We would not travel as a group; he would send us out two by two. We would spread out so as to cover many towns and villages on the way. He gave us authority to tell people the good news of God's community, and assured us that if we had faith, we too could be healers. We were not to take much with us, but to find hospitality as we could along the way. Most of us chose to go with him.

After some time, we all arrived in Judea. Bethany, two miles from Jerusalem, became our headquarters. There was open land for camping, and his friends Martha, Mary, and Lazarus were always hospitable in their large, comfortable home. The women gathered there frequently. Jesus traveled, teaching and preaching in the villages of Judea, as he had in Galilee. At times he went into Jerusalem and preached in one of the courts of the Temple. The priests listened and watched. I saw them, and I was afraid for him.

We celebrated the Passover in Jerusalem, but the seder was a sad meal that year, for we knew that Jesus might be arrested at any time. He knew now that one of his inner circle would betray him. After the meal, Jesus withdrew to a garden on the lower slopes of the Mount of Olives to pray, taking some of his friends with him.

Then Judas came to the garden with Roman soldiers and some of the Temple guards. He kissed Jesus, which was the prearranged sign. The soldiers arrested Jesus. He was tried during the night and condemned to die the next morning. We could not believe it.

The men, mostly simple people from Galilee, were disheartened and afraid without their leader. They were already insecure in this large city. Most of them went into hiding. Even Peter, who had protested that he would follow Jesus to his death, denied that he even knew him when a serving maid questioned him. Women do not have as much to lose. None of us went to bed that night. We kept as close to Jesus as we could, hoping that he could feel our presence and our love and support.

The next morning, exhausted, numb, and grief-stricken, we joined the curious throng walking to the place where crucifixions take place. Most of the women wanted to watch from a distance. I needed to be as close to him as I could, so I made my way through the crowd to where the crosses were being prepared. I found his mother and her sister and Mary, the wife of Clopas, already there. We were soon joined by John, Zebedee's son, the only man among his inner circle with courage enough to be present. He was risking much to be there.

I cannot speak of all that happened. We four women and John clung to each other. We felt the hammer blows in our own flesh. We felt his agony, shared his thirst, and understood when he cried out, "My God, why have you forsaken me?" Hope died there. I felt that God too had died, and the earth as well, for the shock of an earthquake made the ground shudder beneath us. The color left the trees and grass. The sun seemed to die also, and it became as dark as night. The light had gone out of the world.

Sometimes people linger in agony for several days. We were thankful that he did not last long. The light gradually returned, and someone remarked that it was about noon. We wondered how we could bury him properly before the Sabbath began at sundown. Things had happened too quickly to make plans. And truly, none of us had thought he would really die.

Now the crowd made way for a well-dressed, important-looking man. Someone near us said, "That's Joseph, a member of the Sanhedrin." He went to Pilate and asked for the body and was given permission to take it. We were grateful for his courage, for he, like John, was risking much. He spoke to us kindly and said that he too believed in the community of God and tried to live as Jesus taught.

The soldiers lowered the cross to the ground and pulled out the nails. Joseph motioned to a servant to bring up a cart. We helped him wrap the body in a linen shroud that Joseph had brought, and he and John lifted the body onto the cart. Jesus' mother and I asked if we might follow so that we might see where Joseph buried him. He nodded.

Our little procession left the city for the nearby village of Arimathea. In time we came to a lovely garden outside Joseph's home. Here was a cave, newly hewn in a large rock, with a low platform inside. The gardener helped Joseph place the body there, and then they struggled together to roll a heavy stone across the opening of the cave.

It was nearly sundown, the beginning of the Sabbath, so Mary and I hurried back to the city. We were grateful that Joseph had helped us bury him before the Sabbath.

Very early on the first day of the week, while it was still dark, I made my way through the deserted city streets and out to Arimathea. The stars were still visible as I came into Joseph's garden. Even in the dark I could see that the stone was no longer across the opening of the cave. I was panic-stricken. Had grave robbers stolen his beloved body?

I ran back to the city to the house where Peter and the other men were staying. The man who answered my knock said he would wake Peter. After what seemed a long time, Peter and John came out. When I told them the stone had been rolled aside from the entrance to the tomb, the two of them set out running. I ran too, but I could not keep up with them. John is younger than Peter and got there first. He bent down and looked in the cave and saw the linen shroud folded and lying on the bench, and the napkin that covered his head folded in a separate place. Peter came and saw how things were. I saw the fear on their faces. They turned and ran back to the city.

But how could I leave? It was faintly light now. I noticed the gardener already at work, taking advantage of the coolness of the morning. I stooped and looked into the cave. There appeared to be two angels there, and one of them said, "Woman, why do you weep?" And I answered, "They have taken away my teacher, and I do not know where he is." Tears blinded my eyes. I thought I would ask the gardener what he might know. As I turned, I found the gardener already standing there, or so I thought. He too asked why I was weeping. I stammered, "Oh sir, if you have taken him away, tell me where you have laid him."

Then a beloved voice called my name with all the familiar tenderness. I knew him and answered, "Teacher!" He was not wearing his familiar clothes, but rather, I surmised, something that the gardener had given him, for he looked like a work-man. I fell to my knees. I wanted to embrace him, but he stepped back. He told me that we could no longer be together in the flesh as we had been. From now on he would be my Inward Teacher. He told me to be strong to face all that is to come and that he would always be with me, even to the end of the world. He asked me to carry his message to his friends and followers, and added, "Don't forget Peter!"

I will still travel with the others, or by myself, if the men do not want me. I want to bring the good news of the community of God and the assurance that love is stronger than death to people. And as I continue to walk over this lovely earth, I will always be looking for my teacher, for *Christ in the gardener's clothes.*

But first I must find Peter and the others and give them the good news. Will Peter believe me? Will he be bitter that he was not the first to see Jesus after his death? Oh, go with me, Inward Teacher, and help me find *your* presence in the garb of a fisherman.

Comments

There is no evidence in the four Gospels that Mary Magdalene was ever a prostitute. We do not know for sure the nature of her illness. We are told twice, once in Mark 16:9 and again in Luke 8:3, that Jesus had cast out seven demons from her. Demon possession was the common designation for many ill-nesses that could not be otherwise explained. Modern medi-cine with its diagnostic procedures was still many centuries in the future. I think that she probably had epilepsy. Whatever the problem, Jesus had healed her.

Seven demons are not to be equated with seven deadly sins. The woman with a bent-over back had a demon, but there is no suggestion that she was immoral. And the Syrophoenician woman's daughter had a demon, but hardly seems like a sin-ner. Seven is one of those magic numbers storytellers delight to use. I suspect in this case that it indicated her epileptic seizures were severe.

Each of the four Gospel writers gives a different list of women present at the crucifixion. Mary Magdalene is the only one whose name is on all four lists. And all four Gospels report that Jesus appeared first to her after the resurrection, sometimes by herself, sometimes when she was with other women.

We do know that power struggles went on in the movement after Jesus was no longer present in the flesh. The Peter faction eventually won out, and he is counted as the rock on which the church was built. The Gnostic Gospels, ones that were not accepted for the canon of the New Testament, record Peter's jealousy of Mary Magdalene.[1] Whether Peter is to blame for the rumors that she had been a prostitute we do not know. Her prominence in the Jesus movement probably bothered many men and made them want to put her down. The myth is still strongly entrenched today. Ask any group of people what they know about Mary Magdalene, and most of them will tell you that she had been a prostitute.

There are traditions that suggest that Mary was the number-one disciple, and the disciple Jesus loved. Theosophists in India, for example, have the tradition that they were married and had a child. Descendants of that child are always in the world, but we do not know who they may be. Therefore we are to treat all people with love and respect, for anyone may be descended from Jesus and Mary Magdalene.

John's Gospel tells a beautiful story, full of vivid details, of Jesus appearing to Mary on the first Easter morning. I have drawn on it for the closing events of this story.

Reflections

1. There is no evidence in the Gospels that Mary Magdalene was ever a prostitute. What could be the reason people still think that she was?

2. What do you think the "seven demons" that possessed Mary were? How did Jesus cast them out?

3. The Gnostic Gospels record Peter's jealousy of Mary Magdalene. They also add greatly to our knowledge of Jesus and his friends. What could account for their exclusion from the New Testament canon?

4. Why do you think Mary Magdalene mistook Jesus for the gardener? How important are clothes in our identification of people?

5. Jesus entrusted his message and the news of his resurrection to Mary to share with his other friends. Do you think we owe the survival of Christianity to her?

6. Who do you think was "the disciple Jesus loved"?

CHAPTER 12

Mary the Wife of Clopas

John 19:25; Luke 24:13–35

❧

Standing near the cross of Jesus were his mother, and his mother's sister, Mary the wife of Clopas, and Mary Magdalene.

—JOHN 19:25b

Now on that same day two of them were going to a village called Emmaus about seven miles from Jerusalem. . . . Jesus himself came near and went with them, but their eyes were kept from recognizing him. And he said to them, "What are you two discussing with each other while you walk along?" They stood still, looking sad. Then one of them, whose name was Cleopas,[1] answered him, "Are you the only stranger in Jerusalem who does not know the things that have taken place there in these days?"

—LUKE 24:13, 15b–18

The Story of Mary the Wife of Clopas

"Clopas," I said, "let's leave this God-forsaken city. Let's go home." "Yes," he answered, "If we leave soon, we can make it home before dark." It was now midafternoon of the first day of the week. We gathered our things together and took leave of the friends with whom we had stayed for this Passover. They were not as devastated by the events of the last three days as we were. It would be a relief to talk by ourselves, just the two of us, about what had happened.

As we started out, Clopas said it would not be much out of our way to go by the house with the big upper room, where we had eaten the Passover meal. Most of the men from Galilee were staying there, and he wanted to say goodbye to them before they left for their homes up north. He would not be long, he said. I sat down outside the door to wait for him and leaned against the wall of the house. I would have liked to see the women again, too, but most of them were out at Martha's house in Bethany, and that was the opposite direction from Emmaus. We couldn't go there and make it home before dark.

As I waited, I remembered coming to this house just three days ago with all my beloved friends to prepare the seder meal. The day had begun like all Passovers. The men went to the Temple to sacrifice the lambs, and we women went to the market to buy the other things needed for the ritual meal. We divided up the preparation of the meal among us. I volunteered to make the unleavened bread. We worked in thankfulness that God had delivered our people from the oppression of the Egyptians. We prayed that God would deliver Jesus now from the hands of his enemies.

When the men came, we all saw that Jesus was very sad and discouraged. He knew what we did not yet know, that one of his own inner circle of friends would betray him, and that it would happen very soon. The men seemed quarrelsome and confused. Jesus took off his outer garment and tied a towel around his waist. He began to wash the men's feet, and they quieted down. Peter protested loudly that Jesus must not wash his feet, but in the end Jesus washed his also.

The men of the inner circle gathered around the central table in the room, and we women began to serve the meal. I carried in the unleavened bread and placed it before Jesus so that he might bless and break it. I was moved by his strong, yet gentle hands and the grace of his movements. He made breaking the bread not only a holy act, but a beautiful one.

While the men were eating, Jesus said sadly, "One of you is about to betray me." We were all shocked. Men all over the room asked, "Surely, not I?" Jesus responded, "It is one of you Twelve, one who dips bread in the bowl with me." The meal finished in silence. Then we all sang the customary hymn together. Jesus and some of his friends withdrew to the garden called Gethsemane, where he often went to pray. We women cleared off the dishes and food and straightened up the room. Most of the men were staying there and would be back to sleep that night.

Later Clopas told me what happened in the garden. Some of the men closest to Jesus yawned and couldn't keep awake while he prayed. This hurt him. Suddenly Judas, one of the Twelve, came with Roman soldiers and some Pharisees. The occupation army does not have much to do these days, since there is no fighting now. They take out their frustration and boredom on the local population. Judas kissed Jesus, the prearranged sign. Then the soldiers arrested Jesus roughly and dragged him off to the high priest. The men who had been with Jesus were panic-stricken. Most of them left and went into hiding.

Word spread among the women. Most of us went to the high priest's headquarters to try to find out what was happening. We followed along when the high priest sent Jesus to Pilate, who in time condemned him to be crucified in the morning. We hoped Pilate would send him to someone else and that the order would be reversed. Surely Jesus couldn't be tried and sentenced so quickly. We waited anxiously. Finally Pilate sent him to Herod, who had jurisdiction over Galilee and happened to be in Jerusalem at the time. Again we followed along, our hopes rising. But Herod sent him back to Pilate. The condemnation still held.

My major concern was to be with Mary, Jesus' mother. She has been my closest friend since girlhood. I thought of her now, as I waited for Clopas, and tears came to my eyes. Her sister has taken her home with her, away from the city. Otherwise I would not feel free to leave Jerusalem. I wondered what was taking Clopas so long.

I recalled how I met Mary, years ago. I grew up in a town in the hill country, a little northwest of Jerusalem. We had wonderful neighbors next door, an elderly couple who had no children. Zechariah was a priest in the Temple in Jerusalem. His wife, Elizabeth, was a special friend to all the girls growing up in town. She used to tell me stories about Miriam, who helped lead the children of Israel out of bondage in Egypt. Mary is the Greek form of the name "Miriam." I was named for her.

Each Passover season, relatives of Zechariah and Elizabeth came from Galilee and stayed for the week of the Festival of Unleavened Bread. This family had a daughter just my age also named Mary. We became good friends. We used to act out stories about Miriam: Miriam talking to Pharaoh's daughter when she fished her little brother out of the Nile River; Miriam leading the people in singing and dancing when they were all safely across the Red Sea; Miriam finding water as the people traveled across the Sinai Desert toward the Promised Land.

All my other friends wished they had been born boys. Mary thought it was special to be a girl. She was always asking questions, wanting to understand why things are as they are. Each year I looked forward to her coming, and I always learned new things from her.

We grew older. One year we found we were both betrothed, she to Joseph, a carpenter in her hometown, Nazareth in Galilee, and I to Clopas, a shopkeeper in Emmaus, the next town to ours as you go into Jerusalem.

The next year we were both pregnant, but that news was overshadowed by the excitement that Elizabeth was miraculously expecting a baby too, though she was long past the time of childbearing. Our three little boys were all born the same year: Elizabeth's John, Mary's Jesus, and our James.

Our James died of a fever when he was three. Clopas and I hoped for another child, but none was given to us. Both of us hungered for some understanding of the ways of God, some assurance that our son's short life was not meaningless. Was there some purpose to life beyond the daily struggle to keep going?

In time Elizabeth's John came to seem like our son too. We watched him grow into a great prophet. We made the journey several times to hear him preach when he was baptizing people at the ford in the Jordan River. He was powerful and persuasive, but his fierce call to repentance made us somewhat uncomfortable. He seemed to think everyone was wicked and needed to repent. Many did, of course, yet we knew that most people were just trying to survive in an unfriendly world. We could not bring ourselves to go forward to be baptized, yet we continued to go to hear him preach when we could.

We were surprised one day to find that Jesus had come to hear John preach. We talked to him while John was baptizing people and asked him if his message differed from John's. He said John's message was that "the reign of God is at hand." Jesus said he liked to think of it instead as "the community of God," where no one lords it over anyone else. He said he wanted to call his followers "friends" rather than "disciples." He said that the community of God is already here, within us. We may live in it now, even in the midst of Caesar's empire. He told us that the poor, the meek, and the oppressed are special to God and assured us that God loves us and forgives us. When we asked, he said that our spirits do not die when our bodies cease to live.

Clopas and I both felt that this was what we had been waiting to hear all our lives. We felt called to live more fully and not to worry about our sins. From that time on, we looked at Mary's son as our teacher. We tried to live as he taught and we shared his message with our neighbors in Emmaus.

And now it was all over. No miracle had saved Jesus at the last minute. We women had joined the great curious crowd streaming toward Golgotha, "the place of the skull." I went up close to where the crosses were being prepared and joined his mother and her sister. Soon Mary Magdalene came to be with us also. As I sat there now on this first day of the week, waiting for Clopas, I wept as I remembered.

Now Clopas startled me by touching my shoulder. I stood up and leaned against him, still weeping. After a moment I asked him what had taken so long. He said the men had told him that Mary Magdalene had gone to the tomb early this very morning and found the stone rolled away and the tomb empty. Later she said she had seen Jesus alive and that he had asked her to deliver a message to them. The men did not believe her story. It seemed like an idle tale from an overwrought woman.

We walked as we talked and soon reached the Damascus Gate. We paused to look back over the city. Clopas spoke aloud the words that we both remembered hearing Jesus say:

"Jerusalem, Jerusalem, the city that kills the prophets and stones those who are sent to it! How often have I desired to gather your children together as a hen gathers her brood under her wings, and you were not willing!" (Matt. 23:37)

And now we turned our faces homeward on the road to Emmaus. We would have to hurry to make it home before dark. It had been warm during the day, but now a chill wind came up. We pulled the hoods of our cloaks over our heads and held them tightly so they would not blow off. Walking became difficult. The wind seemed to push us back toward the city. I linked my free arm in Clopas's to steady myself. We were both very tired, and we began to argue. Clopas was sure the men were right, that Jesus could not be alive. He said, "You yourself saw him die." And yet I knew without doubt that Mary Magdalene would not make up such a story. I wanted to believe that she had really seen Jesus.

The road had seemed deserted, and yet presently there was another traveler going in our direction. His hood was pulled over his head and we could not see him clearly. I hoped that he would simply pass us and move on. I did not want to make small talk with a stranger. I felt upset that he continued to walk beside us.

Presently he said, "What were you two talking about?" Clopas stopped and blurted out, "Are you the only person in Jerusalem who does not know what has happened?" And the stranger asked, "What happened?" Clopas told him we were talking about Jesus of Nazareth, a great prophet, who had been crucified. He went on to say that some of the women among his followers had found the tomb empty this very morning and were sure that he had risen from the dead, but the men, of course, did not believe their story.

The stranger said that it sounded as if what had happened fulfilled the ancient prophecies. He began quoting passages from the books of Moses and also from the Psalms and the Prophets, explaining what they meant as he talked. Our companion was obviously a rabbi. He quoted the prophet Isaiah:

> He is despised and rejected of men;
> a man of sorrows, and acquainted with grief; . . .
> Surely he hath borne our griefs, and carried our sorrows.
>
> —ISAIAH 53:3a, 4a KJV[2]

"Yes," I said, "that is how it was." Clopas nudged me. It was not proper for a woman to speak to a man she did not know. I had forgotten myself. Jesus always wanted to know what I thought. Clopas would give his opinion on something, and Jesus would say, "But what do you think, Mary?"

Our companion went on with passage after passage. Then I felt that he was speaking directly to me:

> Rejoice greatly, O daughter Zion!
> Shout aloud, O daughter Jerusalem!
> Lo, your king comes to you;
> triumphant and victorious is he,
> humble and riding on a donkey . . .
> he shall command peace to the nations.
>
> —ZECHARIAH 9:9, 10b

I remembered Jesus riding into Jerusalem on a donkey on the day of the Passover. I thought of Mary Magdalene again, and now I somehow felt sure that what she said was true. Jesus was alive again!

Clopas stopped suddenly. We were at Emmaus. We were already at the door of our house. We had been so tired and depressed. Walking had seemed such an effort, but listening to this rabbi had made the miles fly by quickly.

The stranger raised his hand in farewell and started to move on. Clopas said, "Stay with us. The day is far spent." He nodded and we walked into the empty house. Clopas groped for the lamp and I went to the garden in the fading light and found a few vegetables. I could always make unleavened bread. I found a bit of dried fish in the cupboard to add to the vegetables.

While I busied myself with this simple meal, Clopas brought water and washed the feet of our guest. The lamp was dim and flickering. The rabbi was sitting in a dark corner of the room and Clopas could not see his feet clearly. He told me later that the feet felt bruised and sore and that our guest had winced when Clopas rubbed his feet with his towel.

When the meal was ready the men went to the table. I carried the unleavened bread and set it before our learned guest so that he could bless and break it. Tears ran down as I remembered carrying the bread to Jesus at the Passover meal, just three nights before. I wiped my tears with the back of my hand and watched the rabbi take the bread.

Suddenly I knew those hands, those graceful gestures. Then I saw the wounds in the hands. The lamp which had been flickering flared up and illuminated his face. *It was Jesus!* He called us both by name. And then he was gone. He did not rise and go out the door, he simply was no longer there. Perhaps you think this an old woman's tale, but Clopas experienced it too. We stood there amazed. Finally Clopas said, "Did not our hearts burn within us while he talked to us on the road?" I nodded. "Rejoice greatly!" I said.

How could we eat our meal and go to bed as if this were an ordinary homecoming? I put the food away and Clopas extinguished the lamp. We set out in the darkness for Jerusalem, half running in our eagerness.

We found the men still gathered in the upper room. They greeted us with excitement. Peter had also seen Jesus, and everyone acknowledged now that Mary Magdalene had been right. We told them what had happened to us on the road to Emmaus, and how we had known him in the breaking of the bread.

Even as we finished our story, there he was again, in the midst of us, in the familiar room. We all saw him. Some were startled and afraid, remembering how they had hidden in fear while he went to his death. Jesus spoke reassuringly to them. Presently one of the women brought in unleavened bread. He blessed and broke it and passed it to us, saying, "Remember me when you break your bread." And then, once again, he was gone.

In the years since then people have questioned whether his body rose from the dead and was truly with us, or whether it was his spirit that we experienced. And some believe one, and some the other. But I say to you, it does not matter. Love is stronger than death, and those who love are not separated by death. *They live in one another still.*[3]

Comments

1. There were two groups of women at the crucifixion. The first three Gospels all indicate that the women from Galilee stood at a distance watching. Matthew, Mark, and Luke each name several women, a slightly different list in each case, and suggest that there were many more. John, however, gives a list of women standing by the cross, a group especially close to him including his mother and his mother's sister, Mary Magdalene, and another women identified in the Greek as "Mary of Clopas," which English translators

have assumed means "wife of Clopas." Who is this woman in the inner circle who is not mentioned elsewhere?

In the last chapter of Luke, there is a vivid story of two disciples walking back to their home in Emmaus late on the first day of the week, that is, Easter. One of the disciples is called Cleopas and the other is unnamed. Clopas and Cleopas are similar names, although Cleopas is Greek and Clopas is Chaldean. It would be easy to mix up the names. Since neither of the men is mentioned elsewhere in the Bible, some scholars feel that they are really the same man. If Clopas's wife was part of the inner circle of women at the crucifixion, then it seems logical that he would be walking home with her.[4]

2. We do not know the exact location of Emmaus. We are told that it was about seven miles from Jerusalem. At least four villages have been suggested as the original Emmaus, all of them in the hill country west of Jerusalem. In the first chapter of Luke, we are told that Mary "went with haste to a Judean town in the hill country." Was it possible, I speculated, that the two Marys had met and known each other when Mary, the mother of Jesus, visited her kinswoman Elizabeth? Perhaps there had been earlier visits when they were both girls. My story began to fall into place. I introduced this Mary briefly in the first chapter on Elizabeth.

3. The final detail was supplied by the phrase in Luke 24:35 that Jesus became known to them "in the breaking of the bread." Who made the bread that Jesus broke? If Clopas had a wife, obviously she did. Were the hands of Jesus familiar to her from an earlier breaking of the bread, perhaps at that last sad Passover meal?

4. In this story, Jesus appears and disappears arbitrarily. He is there. He is not there, and then again he is there. This suggests a spiritual resurrection rather than an actual physical one. It is something familiar to me, for at times I have been overwhelmed by the presence of some of my own beloved

dead, utterly real and reassuring, but not involving a physical body.

Reflections

1. Who do you think Mary the wife of Clopas was? Do you find the story of her relationship to Mary the mother of Jesus convincing?

2. How have you pictured in your mind the two disciples on the road to Emmaus? Does it seem reasonable to you that it was a husband and wife?

3. Why did they not recognize Jesus on the road? Why did Jesus not identify himself to them at that point?

4. Why do you think they hurried back to Jerusalem in the dark? Was it to confirm Mary Magdalene's story of seeing Jesus?

5. What is your view of the resurrection? Did Jesus return in a human body, as an active spirit, or only in the minds of his followers?

6. Have you ever experienced the presence of someone you loved after death? Was it anything like the experience of Mary and Clopas?

CHAPTER 13

Mary of Bethany

John 11:1–44, 12:1–8; Luke 24:50–51

❦

Six days before the Passover Jesus came to Bethany, the home of Lazarus, whom he had raised from the dead. There they gave a dinner for him. Martha served, and Lazarus was one of those at the table with him. Mary took a pound of costly perfume made of pure nard, anointed Jesus' feet, and wiped them with her hair.

—JOHN 12:1–3a

Then [Jesus] led them out as far as Bethany, and, lifting up his hands, he blessed them. While he was blessing them, he withdrew from them.

—LUKE 24:50–51a

The Story of Mary of Bethany

I was only seven years old, but I fell in love with Jesus the first time I saw him. I did not even know his name yet. I had never seen anyone like him—so full of life, so full of joy, so good to look at, so aware of everything around him. When he looked at me he really saw me. Other people always looked over my head. He made me think I was important, someone he would like to know. He spoke to me, asking my name, and when I told him I was Mary, he said he loved the name; it was his mother's name too. I told him that Lazarus had taught me to read. He asked me what I had read and nodded with approval when I told him. But for the accident of his mother's fainting in front of our house, he would have been just one of the hundreds coming through Bethany on the way to the Passover in Jerusalem, and we would never have known him.

All the people I had known well up until then had either been unwell, like our parents and Lazarus; or overburdened, like my sister Martha; or stiff-necked and joyless, like the men from the synagogue whom our father had asked to handle our money and keep an eye on us. Before Jesus came, there was little for me to look forward to in life. I was getting my education secondhand from Lazarus, and even at seven I grasped things more quickly than he did at twelve. I was trying to avoid helping Martha with her everlasting housework by pretending to be half-sick most of the time. I wanted to be a great scholar and think great thoughts and write great books, but how could I, when I was a girl?

And now everything changed. Although he did not really live with us much of the time, Jesus became part of our family. That made all the difference. Martha became more relaxed about her work and less critical of me. I in turn learned to enjoy helping her and often volunteered to take on some of the chores. And Lazarus grew much stronger and had fewer seizures by his demon.

Jesus usually came for the Passover week and occasionally at other times. I always wanted to be the one to wash his feet after the hot, dusty journey. Then I would curl up beside him and listen to him talk. I was really "sitting at his feet," eagerly learning all I could. I felt so fortunate. Here was a fine scholar, our special friend, who welcomed my attention and my questions and even seemed to value my opinions.

My love for him grew year by year. Of course I knew that the most important thing in his life was to fulfill the mission God had for him. I knew he would probably never marry me.

But I knew also that I could never marry a lesser man. I had given my heart to him, and I could not take it back. Lazarus and Martha understood how I felt and did not press me into marriage.

Jesus began his ministry in Galilee, his home territory. He gathered a group of followers who could eventually take over some of the teaching and healing. Rumor reached us that he was calling women as well as men. We were not surprised. He always treated Martha and me as intelligent human beings, and he treated Lazarus no differently. Hope grew in me. The next time he came, I would ask to be one of his followers and to travel with him too. The Passover was near. I waited eagerly for him to come.

I did not want to tell Martha and Lazarus yet that I wanted to leave home and be one of the followers who traveled with Jesus. When he came I asked that we walk a little way down the road together, so that I could talk to him privately. It never occurred to me that he might turn me down.

And now I learned a lesson in integrity. Jesus told me he doubted that I was strong enough for the rugged life on the road. He said that Martha was concerned about my health and did not press me to do the heavy work. I hung my head. I knew he had seen through my deception all along. I was bitterly disappointed, but I resolved to be sincere in everything I did or said from then on.

Jesus went on to say that I need not travel with him to be his follower. I could be his disciple in Bethany. He said that the community of God can only grow as people who believe in it and understand it live such radiant and loving lives that people want to know the source of their joy. I could live such a life in our family and as I went about errands in Bethany. Increasingly I was the one who went into Jerusalem to carry messages and keep friendships alive. Everywhere I went, he said, I could live the community of God and talk about it when opportunities arose.

And so it happened. People did ask me about the source of my joy, and I began to talk about Jesus and the community of God. A growing group of people, in both Bethany and Jerusalem, began to think of themselves as living in God's community. They were eager to meet Jesus when he came to Judea. (See John 11:45.)

Jesus remained in Galilee for three years, teaching and preaching and healing. Then he knew he must return to Judea, even though it probably meant a confrontation with authorities. Spies had been sent to Galilee to follow his activities there, and we all knew they would be watching him closely now. Our joy that he would be with us was tempered by our concern for his safety.

Many of his Galilean followers came with him. They made their headquarters in Bethany, where they would be less conspicuous than in Jerusalem. Now we met the women among his followers. We invited them to make our home their gathering place. It was a great joy to know these strong, capable, dedicated women who had given their lives to Jesus.

There was one to whom I was especially drawn. She had the same kind of authentic presence that Jesus had, the same vitality and depth of spirit. She too was named Mary, and she came from Magdala, a fishing village in Galilee. I saw that she loved Jesus with the same single-minded devotion that I did. And I saw also that that love was returned in a different way from the love Jesus had for Martha and me. Yet I could not be jealous of her. They were right for each other. I saw also that she was content just to share his life, knowing that God's mission for him must always come first.

The Roman soldiers and spies from the Pharisees always watched while he preached and taught in the villages of Judea now. We learned to pick them out in the crowd and to be aware of what they were doing. From time to time, when things became tense, Jesus withdrew across the Jordan River and preached in towns there. This took him out of the jurisdiction of Pontius

Pilate into that of Herod Antipas, where the danger was less. The authorities in Judea now began to talk openly, not just of arresting him, but of putting him to death. They said he was undermining the whole structure of the laws of Moses.

As Jesus was healing one day in a town in Judea, a spy in the crowd shouted and denounced him for setting aside the Mosaic law. He picked up a stone and threw it, just missing Jesus. Others in the crowd began to throw stones. His friends managed to shield Jesus, and they withdrew quickly to the other side of the river. We only learned of this incident later.

Martha and I hoped we could keep this from Lazarus, but of course we couldn't. Now he became very ill and grew steadily worse. The demon had returned with full force. He lost consciousness for long periods. Through a neighbor who volunteered to find Jesus for us we sent this message to him: "He whom you love is gravely ill."

Our neighbor found Jesus and delivered our message. When he returned he assured us that Jesus would come, but the days dragged on and still he did not appear. Lazarus grew steadily worse. Finally he was unconscious for two whole days. There seemed little hope. Martha and I found the delay difficult to understand. We worried that Jesus would arrive too late.

John, one of the inner circle, still insists that Jesus delayed because he wanted the healing of Lazarus to be a spectacular miracle. He even wrote this later in his book about Jesus. I argued with him that this was unworthy of Jesus. We knew in our hearts that his love for us was greater than that. He would not take advantage of a friend's serious illness and our concern just to show off his power. Later other disciples told us that they were so worried about the recent attempt to stone Jesus that they forcibly detained him. This made more sense to us than John's story.

Lazarus did not regain consciousness, and the physician said he was dead. I hoped that he was still in the grip of the demon. The men from the synagogue insisted that we bury him. As with father, I held out for binding his legs separately so that he could walk out of the cave if the demon left him. I even loosened some of the wrapping over his face before the men came to roll the stone across the entrance to the burial cave, and paid them to leave a small opening at one side.

Martha alternated between grief and hope. She said to me, "Even now I know that God will give Jesus whatever he asks." Now she also told me that she had known with inner certainty the first time we met him, when he was twelve, that he was destined to be the Messiah. Dear Martha! I had childishly fallen in love with him, but she had seen who he really was and lived with that knowledge all these years, as she tried to be his follower.

And still Jesus did not come!

Word of Lazarus's death spread, and friends in Jerusalem now came to mourn with us. Finally someone brought word that Jesus was on his way, and actually quite near. I stayed with the guests while Martha went to meet him. In her anxiety she blurted out what was on both our minds: "If you had been here, our brother would not have died." She told him she had known he was God's chosen one and said she still had faith that he could bring Lazarus back to us. Then she hurried back to the house to be with the guests, so that I could go to meet him too.

I ran, but he was still in the place Martha had left him. Why did he still delay? Tears ran down my face, tears for my beloved brother and tears because I wondered how much Jesus really cared. Like Martha, I told him that if he had come, our brother would still be alive. I gave way to grief and could not control my crying. I looked up and saw that Jesus was weeping too. People in the crowd murmured, "See how much he loved him."

When we walked back to the house together, I asked why he had delayed. He said that he felt, as I did, that Lazarus could come back from the tomb. More than that, however, he had been concerned about his followers, who really felt that if he returned he would be killed. They would not let him return alone and would probably meet their deaths also. He said it was important to him to have some choice as to how and when he might die. He believed God would be his guide in whatever events were to take place.

We reached our house, and Jesus asked some of the men to roll the stone away from the opening of the cave. Dear, skeptical Martha protested, "There will be a stench, Jesus. He's been dead four days." I remembered Father, and how I gave up hope on the fourth day when the odor of death was overpowering.

Jesus ignored her and said in a loud voice, "Lazarus, come forth." We waited breathlessly. Then, to everyone's astonishment, Lazarus did come forth! Martha and I rushed to help him unbind himself and led him into the house, away from all the curious eyes. Martha stirred the fire so that she could warm milk for him to drink.

The crowd went wild. Many insisted on seeing Lazarus for themselves. They kept coming into the house. Several of our neighbors stood at the door to keep them from entering, but the crowd was noisy and would not go away. They kept peering in the windows. Our joy that our brother had come back to us turned into a nightmare.

Lazarus was frightened and very weak. He could not keep even warm milk down. He was still quite cold, and Martha and I rubbed his arms and feet and piled blankets on him. He was confused about what had happened and kept asking for Jesus. Over and over he said, "He called me to come to him. Why has he gone away again?"

Meanwhile Jesus had his own problems. Word of the raising of Lazarus spread rapidly. Many friends from Jerusalem now believed that he was indeed the Messiah and wanted to be his followers. They pressed around him so that he could not move. His friends gradually elbowed people out of the way and they withdrew to Ephraim, a town in the desert on the other side of the river.

Informers went to the Pharisees and told them what had happened. Now the authorities were more determined than ever to do away with him. They called a special meeting of the Sanhedrin, and there was even talk of doing away with Lazarus too.

At times Lazarus said he wished that Jesus had left him in the tomb. It was hard to come back to the frail old body that betrayed him so often. But we coaxed him to eat and gradually he gained a little strength. We watched our beloved brother slowly return to us. He no longer spoke of wishing he were dead. Life stirred in him again, and he began to see the world with new eyes, rejoicing in the miracle of flowers and birds. He began to enjoy the fresh vegetables from the garden that Martha prepared with so much love.

Days passed. As the Passover approached, Jesus returned and told all his friends that he would celebrate it in Jerusalem, in the usual upper room. People tried to talk him out of it, but his mind was made up. Lazarus grew stronger each day and began to seem like himself again. We felt we wanted to celebrate with a quiet dinner for Jesus and his inner circle. Lazarus felt well enough to be at the table. It was just six days before the Passover.

Martha and I planned a simple meal of food that Lazarus could eat and some things we knew Jesus especially enjoyed. Early in the day we shopped at the market for what we did not have in the garden. We found that the fish dealer had fish like those that live in abundance in the Sea of Galilee. Afterwards, on impulse, I bought some expensive ointment, called nard. This was a special occasion.

Jesus was the last to arrive. I washed his feet in the presence of his friends and then rubbed the fragrant nard into them. Out of love I wiped his feet with my hair. Then I got up to help Martha serve the meal.

Judas, the treasurer of the group, complained. If I had so much money, he said, why had I not given it to the poor instead of wasting it on expensive perfume? Jesus rebuked him. The lovely dinner we had planned was not the joyous occasion we had envisioned. People mostly just nibbled at the food, and Lazarus had to leave the table early to go back to his bed.

The Passover was now upon us. Jesus urged us not to try to celebrate it with him in Jerusalem. Lazarus might not be safe there, and the excitement of the city might cause him to become ill again. He said he would come to us when he could. He wanted to think of his family here at home waiting for him, perhaps to give him a place to rest, perhaps to give him sanctuary, perhaps to help him heal from whatever might happen to him. Again he said, "I will come to you. Wait for me."

We could scarcely take in the news that reached us the next day. It just wasn't possible that it was all over. Lazarus fell ill again and said he wished to die too. He refused to eat.

Mary Magdalene came and told us she had seen Jesus alive on the first day of the week. She had messages for all of us. Several people had seen him later, and she was sure he would come to us too.

Days passed, and then one day we heard what sounded like a large group of people coming up the road from Jerusalem. They were singing. Martha and I knew the song and began to sing too:

> Yea, though I walk through the valley of the shadow of death,
> I will fear no evil: for thou art with me.
>
>   —PSALM 23:4a KJV[1]

We ran to the gate and looked down the road. Then the group rounded the last turn before Bethany. And there was Jesus, surrounded by his friends. I think there must have been a hundred people with him. We ran to meet him and fell at his feet. When we came to the entrance to our garden, Jesus stood at the gate and called in a loud voice: "Lazarus, come forth!" In a few minutes Lazarus appeared in the doorway. Seeing Jesus, he ran to him, and Jesus gathered the three of us into his arms.

Jesus led Lazarus into the garden to the shady place under the tree where we had so often been together. Martha and I urged everyone to come in, and even though it was a large group, our garden had room to hold them all. Jesus began to talk. He said we looked like a sizable group in the small space of a garden, but we were only a handful as he thought of the whole world. Yet, he said, the community of God depended on us. Could we live it so contagiously that it would grow and grow until it encompassed the earth, and bring in the age of peace and justice that the prophets had foretold, and for which he had given his life?

Presently he raised his hands in blessing. He said, "And remember, I am with you always." And then he was gone. We did not see him go. He simply was no longer visible to our eyes. We stood silent. Then Mary Magdalene put her arm around Lazarus and said to us all, "He is our Inward Teacher now."

Then someone took up the song they had been singing on the way from Jerusalem. We all joined in as they filed out of the garden and down the road:

> Surely goodness and mercy shall follow me all the
> days of my life:
> And I will dwell in the house of our God forever.
> —PSALM 23:6 KJV[2]

Comments

This was the most difficult of the stories to write. People have such different opinions of Mary that it is hard to visualize her as a person. One writer feels that she lived "in the shadow of her sister."[3] Another characterizes her as "articulating the right praxis of discipleship."[4] A third calls her "a disciple who has a right to learn from Jesus."[5] And a member of my original class at Woodbrooke College argued quite convincingly that she was a mentally retarded adult!

After living with the Bethany family for months and months, I finally concluded that Mary was the brightest one in the family. Martha may have had as much native intelligence, but she was carrying a heavy burden and her mind was occupied with practical matters. Also, she was not educated at the feet of Jesus as Mary was.

Some explanation is needed to account for the story that finally emerged about Mary:

1. Martha's story, which I told four chapters back, was based on the familiar story in Luke. Mary's story is based on two incidents in John's Gospel. The picture of Jesus set forth in John 11 is so at variance with everything else I have learned about Jesus from the Gospels, and so diminishes him in stature, that I cannot accept it. And in writing the story I couldn't force Mary to believe it totally either.

   What are we to make of this passage in John 11:5–6?

   > Accordingly, though Jesus loved Martha and her sister
   > and Lazarus, after having heard that Lazarus was ill, he
   > stayed two days longer in the place where he was.

   And even after he decides to go to Bethany, verse 30 indicates that he dawdles along the way. What kind of love is this for one's worried, anxious friends and their dying brother? Is this the same Jesus who says just four chapters later:

   > "This is my commandment, that you love one another
   > as I have loved you. No one has greater love than this,
   > to lay down one's life for one's friends." (John 15:12–13)

   Finally Jesus does arrive in Bethany, but before raising Lazarus from the dead John reports that he prayed to God thus:

   > And Jesus looked upward and said, "Father, I thank you
   > for having heard me. I know that you always hear me,

but I have said this for the sake of the crowd standing here, so that they may believe that you sent me." (John 11:41–42)

Is this the same Jesus who said,

"And whenever you pray, do not be like the hypocrites; for they love to stand and pray in the synagogues and at the street corners, so that they may be seen by others. Truly I tell you, they have received their reward. But whenever you pray, go into your room and shut the door and pray to your Father who is in secret; and your Father who sees in secret will reward you." (Matt. 6:5–6)

I find it hard to believe that the unconvincing details of this story in John 11 were written by the same author who gave us the vivid account of Jesus' encounter with the woman at the well in John 4, or the tender story of Mary Magdalene's reunion with Jesus on Easter morning in John 20, or the beautiful tale of Jesus fixing breakfast for his friends who have been out fishing all night in John 21.

2. All four Gospels have anointing stories, suggesting that it may have been one incident. There are differences, however. Mark's story is two days before the Passover, while the anointing in John took place six days before. Mary, in John's story, anointed the feet, an act of hospitality. Mark's story is of anointing the head, quite a different thing, as I noted in chapter 10. John's story of Mary anointing the feet of Jesus is included in brief form in this chapter.

3. Finally, I keep finding references to Bethany in the Gospels, such as:

He . . . went out of the city to Bethany, and spent the night there. (Matt. 21:17)

On the following day, when they came from [Bethany], Jesus felt hungry. (Mark 11:12)

(I am tempted to ask why Martha neglected to give him a good breakfast that morning. If she had, he might not have cursed the fig tree!)

Bethany is on the southern slope of the Mount of Olives, and there are many references to his going there. I get the impression that he made his headquarters in Bethany, and surmise that he stayed with Mary and Martha and Lazarus. So I come to the final verses of Luke's Gospel and read:

> Then he led them out as far as Bethany, and lifting up his hands, he blessed them. While he was blessing them, he withdrew from them. (Luke 24:50–51a)

Did Jesus want to include his Bethany family when he took his final leave of his friends? Is this why he led them out "as far as Bethany"?

Reflections

1. What do you make of Mary, Martha's sister? Was she a spoiled brat? mentally retarded? an eager learner sitting at the feet of Jesus? or what?
2. If you had been in Mary's place, would you have helped Martha voluntarily in the kitchen?
3. What do you make of Jesus in chapter 11 of John's Gospel?
4. Do you think Lazarus was really dead, or still in a coma?
5. Do you know anyone who has had a near-death experience, or have you had one yourself? Can you talk about what it was like to return to life again? What impression of life after death do you have?
6. Do the words of Jesus, "Lo, I am with you always, even unto the end of the world," have special meaning today?

CHAPTER 14

Mary the Mother

Matthew 1:16, 18–25, 2:7–23, 12:46–50, 13:54–58; Mark 3:21,
31–35, 6:1–6; Luke 1:26–56, 2:1–52, 8:19–21;
John 2:1–12, 19:23–27; Acts 1:12–14; 2:1–4

❦

Then they returned to Jerusalem from the mount called
Olivet. . . . When they had entered the city, they went to the
room upstairs where they were staying. . . . All these were
constantly devoting themselves to prayer, together with
certain women, including Mary the mother of Jesus, as well
as his brothers.

—ACTS 1:12a, 13a, 14

Mary treasured all these words and pondered them in her
heart.

—LUKE 2:19

The Story of Mary the Mother

After Jesus took his final leave of us all at Bethany, we returned to Jerusalem, singing as we went, still filled with his
inward presence and our love for one another. We gather now
each day in the upper room where we have always celebrated
the Passover, praying together and talking of how we can make
the community of God a reality in Jerusalem.

There is also time for each of us to be alone with our own
thoughts. I have time now to remember all the joy and hurt,
the uncertainty and grief, of my life. I have kept all these things
and pondered them in my heart. Now I need to reflect on it
all, and set down what happened from my own point of view.

This, then, is the story of *my* relationship to my firstborn son.

I remember how frightened I was when I realized that I really was going to have a child. I was only twelve years old, and engaged to Joseph, a respected older man, but the child was not his. If he denounced me when he learned of my condition, I would probably be stoned to death.

I kept going over in my mind a strange dream that I had had. In the dream, the angel Gabriel came to me and said, "Rejoice, highly favored one. God is with you." Now angels are an important part of the spiritual life of our people, but I was puzzled that Gabriel would address someone like me in such a manner. What could it mean? He saw that I was troubled and said, "Do not be afraid. You will give birth to a son and call him Joshua, which means Deliverance." (He is better known now as *Jesus,* the Greek form of his name.) And I answered, "How can this be? I'm not married yet." Gabriel replied that the child was holy, God's child, and added, "With God nothing is impossible." I thought about all this and finally answered, "Let it happen to me as you have said."

At the time, the dream was quite compelling, but later I wondered who would believe me if I told them about it. I knew I had to talk to someone—but who? Not my parents, who had arranged a fine marriage for me. And certainly not Joseph, whom I really did not know yet.

The more I thought about it, I knew it had to be Elizabeth, an older kinswoman to whom I have always been close. But Elizabeth lived in Judea, near Jerusalem, and that is several days' journey from Nazareth in Galilee. I could not make that journey alone. I shuddered when I thought of the Roman soldiers of the occupation army, bored with no war to fight here, and contemptuous of the people in whose country they were stationed. They were everywhere. There were no restraints on what they could do to amuse themselves at the expense of the local people. Young girls were especially vulnerable. The soldiers were particularly eager to find girls who were engaged, but not yet married. No, I would have to travel with a group that included men.

Fortunately, before long we learned that neighbors planned a trip to Jerusalem for a wedding. My mother asked if I might travel with them. Elizabeth was going to have a child, although she was past that stage of her life. My mother felt I could be of help to her and said I might stay until the child was born, about three months. Neither of my parents seemed aware of my own condition.

Elizabeth knew, however, even before I told her. Her response was more than I could have hoped for. She made me believe in the dream. She helped me feel that I could face the world with confidence, and that all would be well.

We talked of the children we were carrying. Elizabeth's child was very active now, and at times his movements seemed quite violent. She thought he would be "a voice crying in the wilderness," always in conflict with the sinful world into which he was coming. She encouraged me to think about the message my child would bring to the world. Surely, I thought, he would preach justice and peace, like our great prophets. I hoped he would be on the side of the poor, the heavily burdened, and those of low degree. Elizabeth felt that women and children would be important to him.

She told me I had a responsibility, an opportunity really, to provide my child with the education and understanding he would need to grow into a powerful voice for God's righteousness and truth. She reminded me that I was unusually prepared to be his mother. My parents had no sons, and my father treated me and my sister like sons, teaching us to read and write and providing us with a solid foundation of knowledge of the scriptures. Our mother sang to us the great songs of our people and told us their stories. We knew about the women as well as the men. Elizabeth said that it would be important for me to pass all this knowledge on to my son.

The miracle happened! Joseph married me! Gabriel visited him in a dream also, telling me I was carrying a holy child.

He was a kind and righteous man and did not question or reproach me. And so I took up my life as the carpenter's wife.

The townspeople of Nazareth, however, were not so magnanimous. As I went back and forth to the well, women stared at me curiously. I knew I was the subject of their gossip. I held my head high and greeted them all courteously and confidently. Joseph was an excellent carpenter and his business did not suffer. People did not gossip or ask questions about me in his presence.

Before my son was born, a decree went out from Caesar Augustus for a census. People were to enroll in their home cities, and for Joseph this meant Bethlehem, since he was of the lineage of David the King. With luck we might be back before the baby came, but I really hoped he would be born in Bethlehem. And that happened! The city was very crowded and there was no room for us at the inn. The innkeeper offered us the use of a cave used as a stable behind the inn, and there my son was born, with friendly beasts looking on. I thought I heard angels singing.

And I sang to my precious little son. I sang Hannah's song when she had given birth to Samuel, but I changed it so that it was my song too:

> My spirit rejoices in you, O God,
> for you have looked with favor on the lowliness of your
>   servant. . . .
> You, the Mighty One, have done great things for me and holy
>   is your name. . . .
> You have scattered the proud in the thoughts of their hearts.
> You have brought down the powerful from their thrones, and
>   lifted up the lowly;
> You have filled the hungry with good things, and sent the rich
>   away empty.
>
>   —LUKE 1:46–48, 49–53[1]

And I sang to him all the songs of David the King, mile after mile, as we fled to Egypt, for we had learned that Herod saw him as a threat to his power and would try to do away with *my* child who had been born in a stable! Herod did not live long after we arrived in Egypt. When we heard of his death, we returned to Nazareth.

Joseph had faithfully kept away from me until Jesus was weaned, but now the other children began to come, first James, and then Joseph, whom we sometimes called Joses to distinguish him from his father. I told Jesus stories as I worked and cared for the other children, stories of the great women and men of our people, Sarah and Abraham, Rebekah and Isaac, and Leah and Rachel and Jacob. The younger children listened too when they grew old enough. By that time I was teaching Jesus to read and write and to memorize some of the great passages of our scripture.

But the children kept coming, more sons, and daughters too. I was hard-pressed to teach Jesus all that I wanted to, because of the overload of work and the exhaustion of constant childbearing. Sometimes Joseph accused me of favoring Jesus over the other children. The idea that I was the mother of a holy child seemed like a faraway girlish dream to him now, something I should have outgrown.

My children are all dear to me. I often wished that I had had the time and, more important, the strength, to treat each of them as a special gift from God. But I did keep on teaching Jesus, and including the others as I could. They all learned to read and write, and they all know a fair amount of scripture. Jesus learned quickly and soon could work on his own. He kept asking me questions, which I couldn't always answer. Often he figured things out for himself.

One day he came back from an errand in town. He was eleven now, almost a man. He said the boys had taunted him that Joseph was not really his father. He wanted to know the truth. I took a deep breath and told him it was true. Of course he wanted to know who his father was. I told him of the dream, and said that he was a holy child, a child of God. He looked at me in amazement and asked, "You mean *God* is my father?" Without waiting for my answer he said, "Then God really is my *Abba* (Daddy)!" I told him that for now this must be our secret. I warned him not to talk about it to the boys of the town.

Jesus worked with Joseph in the carpentry shop and learned the trade well. He had a feel for wood and a sense of the people who would use the things he made. His yokes were in great demand. He was conscious of the beasts who would be yoked together. He said that if the yoke was easy on the shoulders, the burden would seem lighter, and the oxen could go farther without exhaustion. Joseph was pleased that Jesus had an aptitude for wood, for none of the other boys seem to have it. Aware of Joseph's hope that he would take over the business some day, Jesus confided in me that he did not want Joseph counting on him. God had other plans for him. I told him I understood that, but that I hoped he would try not to hurt Joseph.

Jesus turned twelve. My mother offered to care for the younger children so that Joseph and I could both go with Jesus to Jerusalem for the Passover that would mark his becoming a man. It was a happy week with Elizabeth and her John. It was also the time we met Martha and her family in Bethany.

When it was time to start home, Jesus told us not to wait for him, that he still had people he wished to see. We told him to meet us where the Nazareth group planned to camp for the night and thought no more about it. After all, he was grown now. But when evening came, we went from campfire to campfire without finding him. We hastily returned to Jerusalem to look for him. After two days, we finally found him at the Temple, asking questions of a group of scholars who seemed amazed at his understanding.

Now that we had finally found him, anxiety gave way to annoyance and I blurted out, "Child, why have you done this to us? Your father and I have been searching for you anxiously." Too late I saw the look of hurt on his face. He was a man now, no longer a child. I would have given anything to take back my careless word. Somewhat coldly he asked, "Why were you searching for me? You should have known that I would be in my Father's house." And now I saw the look of hurt pass over Joseph's face.

In the end he came back home with us. He had found he could not manage on his own yet in Jerusalem. He lived in the house with us and worked with Joseph in the shop. At times I felt the old closeness between us. At other times, with all the pressures of a large, growing family, I was too exhausted to say the right things.

Yet he did not leave home officially for eighteen years. People often ask me what he did during all that time. It was an age of travel. Alexander had conquered everything, all the way to India, and had built a fine system of roads to keep his vast empire together. And the Romans had gone all the way to Britain off the coast of the northern lands. From time to time, Jesus packed his tools and took off, knowing he could support himself along the way with his skill as a carpenter. He did travel to India and talked to holy men in the mountains there. This helped shape his message of love and nonresistance to evil and violence.

Another time he traveled by ship to Britain. Each time he came home, he enchanted us all with tales of his adventures and descriptions of strange places and people. He was a wonderful storyteller. I watched him grow during this time, not only in knowledge of the world, but in wisdom and in the ability to express himself forcefully.

Now we heard that Elizabeth's son John had begun preaching in Judea, near the ford in the Jordan River. He called people to repent and then baptized them. Jesus told us he must go to

Judea to hear John and that he would not be back to work in the shop with Joseph. I saw sadly that I must let him go, not just physically, but in my heart as well.

Herod arrested John and eventually put him to death. He had his eye on Jesus also, and Jesus decided to begin his ministry here in Galilee. Four young men came back with him, his first disciples. They all arrived at our house one day.

And now there occurred a series of events painful to remember. The five young men went with me to the wedding of a cousin in Cana. More people had come than they expected, and I saw that the wine was giving out. I mentioned this to Jesus, believing he might help, but he responded coldly, "Woman, what does this have to do with me?" It hurt to be addressed with the impersonal word "woman" when I am his mother. In the end he did provide them with more wine.

And on the Sabbath we all went to the synagogue. Jesus went to the front and asked for the scroll of Isaiah. He read and commented beautifully, and I was so proud of him. Surely his greatness would be apparent to everyone. But no! I heard people saying, "Where does he get all this wisdom? Isn't this the carpenter? Isn't he Mary's son?" Calling him "Mary's son" when Joseph was there with him in the synagogue revived the old scandal of his origin. Others looked around the room and pointed out his brothers, saying, "Are not his brothers James and Joseph, Judas and Simon? And his sisters are here too!" Jesus raised his voice above the clamor and said, "Prophets are not without honor except in their hometowns." The crowd became angry and drove him out of the village. I went home and could not be comforted. It did not help that Joseph thought Jesus had brought it on himself.

Nor is that all. Jesus now made his headquarters in Capernaum. Word of him trickled back to Nazareth from time to time. Enormous crowds followed him everywhere, and people said he was casting out demons, which must mean he was in league with the devil. There were rumors that he was out of his mind. His brothers were upset by all the gossip about him and decided to find him and somehow restrain him. After some days they returned without having had a chance to speak to him because of the great crowds. They said people obviously loved him. They had seen him heal several people, and he did not act like someone in league with the devil.

Time went by. Joseph arranged marriages for our daughters. His health began to fail, and finally he died. And now after all the busy years, I found myself with time on my hands. What was God calling me to do with the rest of my life? I was ready to leave narrow-minded Nazareth, but where could I go? What could I do? James and Joseph were still at home with me. And they too wondered what to do with their lives. We talked about it endlessly, and while we talked I began weaving a tunic for my eldest son, making it seamless, woven in one piece from top to bottom. I dyed it blue, his favorite color, and I embroidered borders of golden birds around the neck and hem. When it was finished, James and Joseph suggested that we take it to him.

We walked all the way to Capernaum, hoping he would be there. People pointed out his house, and from the crowd gathered around it, we knew he must be at home. We sent word in to him that his mother and brothers would like to see him. His voice carried to us outside, "Who is my mother? and who are my brothers? Those who do the will of God are my brothers and sisters and mother." We stood there, not knowing what to do.

Presently he came out of the house, but he did not seem to see us or acknowledge our presence. He headed up the hill to an open place with a rise of ground from which he could speak to the crowd that was gathering. We followed along, and we heard him begin:

Blessed are the poor in spirit . . .
"Blessed are those who mourn, for they will be comforted.
"Blessed are the meek, for they will inherit the earth.
"Blessed are those who hunger and thirst for righteousness,
    for they will be filled.

"Blessed are the merciful, for they will receive mercy.

"Blessed are the pure in heart, for they will see God.

"Blessed are the peacemakers, for they will be called children
   of God."

—MATTHEW 5:3–9

As I listened to these words, I remembered my dreams for
him before he was born. This was the message I had hoped he
would preach. I knew now that what I really wanted was to
become his follower. And I knew at the same time that he was
not likely to accept me. I turned away from the crowd and
began to cry. Mary Magdalene saw me. She came and put her
arm around me and led me to a place away from the crowd
where we could talk. I poured out my story to her. She helped
me understand that Jesus could not let his family lay special
claims on him and so perhaps stand in the way of his fulfilling
God's mission for him. I realized that that was true, that out of
worry for his safety, I might try to talk him out of some course
of action he had to take. He was not only my child, but God's,
and God must always come first. I realized also that if his
mother were one of his disciples, others might try to reach
him through her.

Mary understood how it hurt when he called me "woman"
so impersonally. She said that as God's child, he must love all
people as God loves them. God sends his rain on the just and
the unjust, on family and on strangers. Jesus could not love
his birth family more than he loved the whole human family.

Now James and Joseph joined us. They said they also really
wanted to be his disciples, to be part of the group not as his
brothers, but as those convinced of his message. Mary pointed
out the difficulties in our being part of the group, if it were
generally known we were of his family. I told her that if I could
join the followers, it would be as "the mother of James and
Joseph," not as the mother of Jesus. There were so many women
named Mary that each one had to have some additional identification. I asked her to take him the tunic I had made and to

tell him that it was a gift from Mary the mother of James and Joseph.

We waited while she went to him. When she could speak to him privately, she told him all that we had said, and then he himself came and joined us. "Can you let me drink the cup that I must drink?" he asked. "Can you be sure you will not try to dissuade me from whatever is God's will for me? Can you follow me wherever I must go?" He asked us to think about it for several days and then come back. In the end, we honestly felt we could do what he asked. We became his disciples, and no one ever mentioned that we were part of his original family, although many must have known. I was always known as "Mary the mother of James and Joseph."

And now I became part of that wonderful group of women disciples. I felt that I had come home at last, that this was indeed where I belonged. I was the eldest, and they accepted me quickly. They always wanted to know what I thought, and I began to tell them the stories of the great women of our heritage—Hannah and Huldah and Deborah, and all the others.

When Jesus set his face to return to Jerusalem, we went with him. We watched events unfold that fateful Passover week. When he came for that final sad seder meal, I saw that he was wearing the seamless tunic I had made for him. That was what he was still wearing when he went to his death.

Now I saw that James and Joseph were determined to stand by Jesus, and I pled with them with all the persuasion I had. I told them I knew I had to lose *one* son, but I begged them to go into hiding and stay out of sight so that I would not lose *three* sons. Wanting to be loyal to Jesus, they held out quite a while against me. In the end I prevailed, and they went with the other men into hiding. Now I realized that Jesus had been right in exacting the promise from me, for had I not promised, I would have pled with him too.

John, one of the earliest of his disciples, stood with my sister and me and the other two Marys at the foot of the cross. At one point Jesus turned his head toward us and said to me,

"Woman, behold your son," and then to John, "Behold your mother." John put his arm around me. That in his agony Jesus was concerned to provide for me seemed somehow to restore the bond between us and wipe out my grief for the years when I felt I could not reach him. That he still called me "woman" did not matter.

There is no sorrow like losing a child. Children ought to outlive their parents so that there is an orderly procession from generation to generation. I remembered that when we took Jesus as a baby eight days old to the Temple, an elderly woman there said to me, "A sword will pierce through your own soul."

In the days that followed, he came to me, as he did to the others. He no longer called me "woman," but by my name, Mary. He told me that there were two things he hoped I would do to help his followers establish the community of God, so that his message would not perish from the earth. He said that many of his disciples lacked a grounding in our great heritage. He asked me to be their teacher, to tell them the great stories, to teach them the beautiful songs, and to explain the scripture to them, as I had done for him when he was a boy. In addition he hoped I would help to hold the small community of God in Jerusalem together, loving them all as he loved them, and never giving up on them, no matter how stubborn and unloving they might be at times. And finally he spoke of his love for me and his gratitude that I could let him go.

We returned to Jerusalem, after his final blessing at Bethany. We have gathered each day in the upper room in silent waiting and prayer. Suddenly one day we all felt the power of God come upon us. It seemed like tongues of flame enveloping each one of us, and we knew we were being commissioned to carry on the work of Jesus and to proclaim his message. We found we could speak in various languages, able to reach the diverse people of this cosmopolitan city. We felt our youth renewed; we were able to run and not be weary.

There are about one hundred twenty of us in the Jerusalem community. We live very simply, sharing all things in common. Some are called to preach; some to heal; and others to visit the poor and the sick, the widows and the fatherless. I teach them, as Jesus asked of me. Even the men are willing to accept my instruction now and are learning eagerly.

More important, I carry the dream of helping this fragile community of God in Jerusalem to flourish and grow strong. I want to help hold it together, as we all face the difficulties and dangers of living in an occupied city, a city that felt so threatened by the message of love and forgiveness brought by Jesus that they finally put him to death.

These days, I find words of the prophet Isaiah speaking to me:

> Comfort ye, comfort ye my people, saith your God.
> Speak ye comfortably to Jerusalem, and cry unto her,
> that her warfare is accomplished, that her iniquity is
> pardoned.
>
> —ISAIAH 40:1–2a KJV[2]

Even so, let it be.

Comments

In writing this chapter, I have tried to let go of "Mary the mother of God," the woman of the little statues in gardens, with the half-smile and outstretched arms, dressed in blue. As I have done with each of the other women, I have worked on this story by immersing myself in the Gospels, trying to put together Mary's story from the glimpses of her, the hints about her, the bits and pieces of conversation by her and others that I found in the various translations of the Gospels, and going back to my Greek testament. What I found needs some explanation:

1. For two thousand years, Mary has been presented as an unattainable role model for girls: the mother who had a

baby without sex and who still remains a "virgin." In this age when teenage pregnancies are not uncommon, I want to present Mary as a different kind of role model: the inner-directed woman who does not take her passive identity from men, but is an autonomous human being. In her book *Women's Mysteries,* Christine Downing suggests a different meaning for the word "virgin." She says that a woman, whether married or not, whose "center is in herself" is a virgin. She is not dependent on men for her identity.[3]

We have hints that Mary was such a woman: she wonders about the angel Gabriel's manner of addressing her, and she questions his saying that she will have a child when she is not yet married. And in the end, she gives *her* assent, that things shall happen as he says.

2. It was shocking to me at first to find that there is no record of a kind word spoken by Jesus to his mother in any of the four Gospels. Then I came to understand why. Jesus too must be autonomous. He must do what he perceives the will of God to be for him. His relation to his family, and his mother in particular, involves separating himself from them lest they make claims of affection on him that will keep him from doing and being what he must do and be. God's mission is the only thing that matters.

Jesus must keep his mother at arm's length so that she cannot project her concern for his safety onto him. It is more important for each of us to be the person we were meant to be and do the things we are called to do than to maintain a close family relationship, painful as that may be for everyone involved.

3. I see Mary as a role model not only for teenage girls, but for older women as well. As Luke reports in the first chapter of Acts, with her children grown and gone and her husband no longer living, she became an active member of the group that carried on the work of Jesus. She was present at Pentecost, when the power came down, and by the life expectan-

cies of that day, she must have been an old woman. Yet
tradition tells us she lived fifteen years in the Jerusalem
community of Christians after Pentecost.

4. Ann Johnson, in her book *Miryam of Jerusalem, Teacher of
the Disciples*, speaks of a tradition of Mary as teacher of the
apostles in the early church. In the basilica of St. Mary
Major in Rome, she can be seen sitting with a scroll on her
knees and Peter and Paul and others sitting at her feet.

Johnson also speaks of the tradition of Mary as scholar,
learning from her parents as a child. She is also said to have
been the primary teacher of Jesus, a tradition that Johnson
says was suppressed when Constantine became emperor in
the fourth century and Christianity became an official religion.[4]

5. Since we know that Jesus wanted to leave his family at age
twelve, it is difficult to understand his waiting eighteen years
to make the final break. When my husband and I visited
York, England, we found the legend that Jesus had been
there as a carpenter as a young man very much alive. Beneath the great York Minster is the foundation of a building
dating back to the time of Jesus, and there is a strong tradition that he had worked on that building. The tradition of
his having been in England is also alive at Glastonbury. This
came to the fore when the new discipline of archeology discovered and identified the Roman ruins. William Blake, fas-
cinated by this possibility, wrote his beautiful poem:

And did those feet in ancient time
Walk upon England's mountains green?
And was the holy Lamb of God
On England's pleasant pastures seen?
And did the Countenance Divine
Shine forth upon our clouded hills?
And was Jerusalem builded here
Among these dark Satanic Mills?

Bring me my bow of burning gold!
Bring me my arrows of desire!
Bring me my spear! O clouds, unfold!
Bring me my chariot of fire!
I will not cease from mental fight,
Nor shall my sword sleep in my hand,
Till we have built Jerusalem
In England's green and pleasant land.[5]

Traditions also exist that he traveled to India and studied with holy men in the Himalayas. The thrust of his message is certainly different from the prevailing point of view in our Western tradition. Jesus advocated nonviolence, voluntary poverty, and humility. These are strongly emphasized in Hinduism, Buddhism, and other Eastern religions. They stand in sharp contrast to the prevailing violence, "might makes right" attitude, greed, and consumerism of much of our Western society, including parts of the Christian church.

6. John records that Mary the mother was present at the crucifixion. If so, why do not the other Gospels mention it? I am indebted to Judith Applegate, a New Testament scholar, for the following insight.[6] Matthew, Mark, and Luke each present somewhat different lists of the women present, but each includes a woman who is known variously as "Mary the mother of James and Joseph," "Mary the mother of James," or "Mary the mother of Joses." You come to feel it is the same woman. Since James and Joseph are listed as his brothers by his hostile fellow townspeople when he preaches in Nazareth, some scholars now feel that these references are to Mary the mother of Jesus, and that she joined the disciples as "Mary the mother of James and Joseph."

7. Finally, Matthew records that Gabriel appeared to Joseph "in a dream." I reason from this that perhaps that is how he appeared to Mary. I found I wasn't able to describe convincingly a real angel appearing to Mary!

Reflections

1. What meaning does Mary have for you?
2. Jesus appears to be a very precocious young man who felt the independence of manhood important. How should his mother have dealt with him at age twelve?
3. Did you experience the adolescent need for independence in your life? in your children's lives?
4. The author has suggested one possible explanation of what Jesus did between the ages of twelve and thirty. Does it seem plausible? What else might he have done during that time?
5. Why do you think Jesus called his mother "woman," and seemed to distance himself from her? Is the author's explanation convincing? What other reasons might there be?
6. Do you think Mary joined the disciples as "the mother of James and Joseph"? Would this have protected Jesus, since some of the other disciples must have known that she was also the mother of Jesus?
7. The Roman Catholic Church has determined not only that Jesus was "immaculately conceived" but that Mary was also. Are these assumptions necessary for a full appreciation of the nature of Jesus?
8. One tradition has Mary living in the Jerusalem community of Christians after the resurrection. Another has her going to Ephesus with John, the disciple to whom Jesus entrusted her. Is there any reason for preferring one tradition over the other? Could she have done both?

Notes

❦

Preface

1. Nancy Mairs, *Ordinary Time: Cycles in Marriage, Faith, and Renewal* (Boston: Beacon Press, 1993), 180ff.

2. Walt Whitman, "Out of the Cradle Endlessly Rocking," in *Leaves of Grass*, ed. Harold W. Blodgett and Sculley Bradley (New York: W. W. Norton, 1965), 247.

3. Ursula Le Guin, "She Unnames Them," *New Yorker*, 21 January 1985.

6. The Syrophoenician Woman

1. I have used the Revised Standard Version here, rather than the New Revised Standard Version, since the RSV calls the woman a Greek, which is an accurate translation of the original Greek, *hellenis*. The NRSV calls her a Gentile.

2. I have used the King James Version here for its beauty and familiarity. It seemed right to me.

7. The Mother of the Sons of Zebedee

1. I have substituted the word "God" as less gender-specific than "the Lord," used in most translations of this passage. In addition, it makes the line scan properly, thus enhancing Isaiah's poetry.

2. This passage appears in the past tense in John's Gospel. I have put it into the present tense, since in this story John has not yet written his Gospel.

8. The Bent-over Woman

1. For the grandmother's insights on pain, I am indebted to Marti Lynn Matthews, *Pain: The Challenge and the Gift* (Walpole, N.H.: Stillpoint Press, 1991).

9. Martha

1. See Henri J. M. Nouwen, *The Wounded Healer* (Garden City, N.Y.: Doubleday, 1972), 91–93.
2. "Guests of My Life," title of a poem by Rabindranath Tagore, in *Crossing* (London: Macmillan, 1921), no. 75. See also Elizabeth Watson, *Guests of My Life* (Burnsville, N.C.: Celo Press, 1977); (Philadelphia: Friends General Conference, 1996, fifth printing).

10. The Woman Who Anointed Jesus

1. Elisabeth Schüssler Fiorenza, *In Memory of Her: A Feminist, Theological Reconstruction of Christian Origins* (New York: Crossroad, 1983), xiv.
2. Elisabeth Moltmann-Wendel, *The Women around Jesus* (New York: Crossroad, 1982), 98–99.
3. Starhawk, *The Spiral Dance* (San Francisco: Harper & Row, 1979), 32.

11. Mary Magdalene

1. Elaine Pagels, *The Gnostic Gospels* (New York: Random House, 1979), 64ff.

12. Mary the Wife of Clopas

1. Note the first section under Comments.
2. I have used the King James version here, for its familiarity and beauty, and also because it uses the word "griefs" for what the NRSV translates "infirmities." I think Jesus suffered more from grief than from infirmities.
3. William Penn, *Some Fruits of Solitude*, 1693, no. 131, in a section called "Reflections and Maxims."
4. I am indebted to Anne Thomas, a Canadian biblical scholar, who some years ago suggested to me that Clopas and Cleopas were the same man, and that the other person on the road to Emmaus was a woman, Mary the wife of Clopas.

13. Mary of Bethany

1. I have used the King James Version here because of its familiarity and beauty. Modern translations make prose out of the Psalmist's poetry.
2. I have substituted the words "our God" as less gender-specific than "the Lord," used in virtually all translations.
3. Moltmann-Wendell, *The Women around Jesus*, 53.
4. Fiorenza, *In Memory of Her*, 330.
5. Ben Witherington III, *Women in the Ministry of Jesus* (Cambridge: Cambridge University Press, 1984), 115.

14. Mary the Mother

1. I have used direct address in this quotation from the Magnificat, as being appropriate in this story.

2. I have used the King James Version here for its familiar beauty.

3. Christine Downing, *Women's Mysteries* (New York: Crossroad, 1993), 13.

4. Ann Johnson, *Miryam of Jerusalem, Teacher of the Disciples* (Notre Dame, Ind.: Ave Maria Press, 1991), 1ff.

5. William Blake, opening lines of the long poem *Milton*. From *The Oxford Book of English Verse, 1250–1918*, ed. Sir Arthur Quiller-Couch (Oxford: Oxford University Press, 1940), 574.

6. I met and talked with Judith Applegate at a women's theological conference in England in 1990. At that time she was teaching New Testament at the Earlham School of Religion, Richmond, Indiana.

Selected Bibliography

❧

References

In addition to the standard Bible commentaries, some of which were too patriarchal in their point of view to be much help, I made much use of the following references:

Achtemeier, Paul J., gen. ed. *Harper's Bible Dictionary.* San Francisco: Harper & Row, 1985.

Gold, Victor Roland, et al., eds. *The New Testament and the Psalms: An Inclusive Version.* New York: Oxford University Press, 1995.

Gospel Parallels: A Synopsis of the First Three Gospels. Text used: The Revised Standard Version. New York: Thomas Nelson & Sons, 1949.

May, Herbert G., ed. *Oxford Bible Atlas.* 3d ed. New York: Oxford University Press, 1984.

Metzger, Bruce M., and Michael D. Coogan, eds. *The Oxford Companion to the Bible.* New York: Oxford University Press, 1993.

Morrison, Clinton. *An Analytical Concordance of the Revised Standard Version of the New Testament.* Philadelphia: Westminster Press, 1979.

Newsom, Carol A., and Sharon H. Ringe, eds. *The Women's Bible Commentary.* Louisville, Ky.: Westminster/John Knox Press, 1992.

Rousseau, John J., and Rami Arav. *Jesus and His World: An Archaeological and Cultural Dictionary.* Minneapolis: Fortress Press, 1995.

Priests for Equality. *The Inclusive New Testament.* Brentwood, Md.: Priests for Equality, 1994.

Strong, James, *The New Strong's Exhaustive Concordance of the Bible.* Nashville: Thomas Nelson, 1990.

Throckmorton, Burton H., Jr., trans. and ed. *The Gospels and the Letters of Paul: An Inclusive-Language Edition.* Cleveland: The Pilgrim Press, 1992.

Books Cited in the Text

Downing, Christine. *Women's Mysteries.* New York: Crossroad, 1992.

Fiorenza, Elisabeth Schüssler. *In Memory of Her: A Feminist Theological Reconstruction of Christian Origins.* New York: Crossroad, 1983.

Johnson, Ann. *Miryam of Jerusalem, Teacher of the Disciples.* Notre Dame, Ind.: Ave Maria Press, 1991.

Mairs, Nancy. *Ordinary Time: Cycles in Marriage, Faith, and Renewal.* Boston: Beacon Press, 1993.

Matthews, Marti Lynn. *Pain: The Challenge and the Gift.* Walpole, N.H.: Stillpoint Press, 1991.

Moltmann-Wendel, Elisabeth. *The Women around Jesus.* New York: Crossroad, 1982.

Nouwen, Henri J. M. *The Wounded Healer.* Garden City, N.Y.: Doubleday, 1972.

Pagels, Elaine. *The Gnostic Gospels.* New York: Random House, 1979.

Starhawk. *The Spiral Dance.* San Francisco: Harper & Row, 1979.

Witherington, Ben, III. *Women in the Ministry of Jesus.* Cambridge: Cambridge University Press, 1984.

A Personal Selection of Other Relevant Books

Borg, Marcus J. *Meeting Jesus Again for the First Time: The Historical Jesus and the Heart of Contemporary Faith.* San Francisco: Harper San Francisco, 1995.

Collins, Adela Yarbro, ed. *Feminist Perspectives on Biblical Scholarship.* Atlanta: Scholars Press, 1985.

Crossan, John Dominic. *The Historical Jesus: the Life of a Mediterranean Jewish Peasant.* San Francisco: Harper San Francisco, 1991.

Fredricksen, Paula. *From Jesus to Christ: The Origin of the New Testament Images of Jesus.* New Haven: Yale University Press, 1988.

Funk, Robert W. *Honest to Jesus: Jesus for a New Millennium.* San Francisco: Harper San Francisco, 1996.

The Gospel of Thomas: The Hidden Sayings of Jesus. New translation with introduction and notes by Marvin Meyer. Interpretation by Harold Bloom. San Francisco: Harper San Francisco, 1992.

Helms, Randel. *Gospel Fictions.* Buffalo: Prometheus Books, 1988.

Mack, Burton L. *The Lost Gospel: The Book of Q and Christian Origins.* San Francisco: Harper San Francisco, 1993.

Mitchell, Stephen. *The Gospel According to Jesus.* New York: HarperCollins, 1991.

Mollenkott, Virginia Ramey. *The Divine Feminine; The Biblical Imagery of God as Female.* New York: Crossroad, 1983.

Mounce, Robert H. *Matthew: A Good News Commentary.* San Francisco: Harper & Row, 1985.

Nolan, Albert. *Jesus before Christianity.* Maryknoll, N.Y.: Orbis Books, 1978.

Nunnally-Cox, Janice. *Foremothers: Women of the Bible.* New York: Seabury Press, 1981.

Pelikan, Jaroslav. *Jesus through the Centuries.* New Haven: Yale University Press, 1986.

Robinson, James M., gen. ed. *The Nag Hammadi Library in English.* San Francisco: Harper & Row, 1977.

———. *The Problem of History in Mark, and Other Marcan Studies.* Philadelphia: Fortress Press, 1982.

Ruether, Rosemary Radford. *Mary—The Feminine Face of the Church.* London: SCM Press, 1979.

———. *To Change the World: Christology and Cultural Criticism.* New York: Crossroad, 1981.

Theissen, Gerd. *The First Followers of Jesus: A Sociological Analysis of the Earliest Christianity.* London: SCM Press, 1978.

Wahlberg, Rachel Conrad. *Jesus According to a Woman* New York: Paulist Press, 1975.

Winter, Miriam Therese. *WomanWord: A Feminist Lectionary and Psalter—Women of the New Testament.* New York: Crossroad, 1991.